UNMASKING MONSTERS

UNMASKING MONSTERS

CHOOK HENWOOD

ALLEN&UNWIN
AUCKLAND·SYDNEY·MELBOURNE·LONDON

First published in 2024

Copyright © David Henwood 2024

Allen & Unwin
Level 2, 10 College Hill, Freemans Bay
Auckland 1011, New Zealand
Phone: (64 9) 377 3800
Email: auckland@allenandunwin.com
Web: www.allenandunwin.co.nz

83 Alexander Street
Crows Nest NSW 2065, Australia
Phone: (61 2) 8425 0100

A catalogue record for this book is available from
the National Library of New Zealand.

ISBN 978 1 991006 85 1

Cover design: Luke Causby/Blue Cork
Internal design: Kate Barraclough
Set in Adobe Caslon Pro
Printed and bound in Australia by the Opus Group

10 9 8 7 6 5 4 3 2 1

For my wife Carolyn and my special extended family;
My band of brothers and sisters from the Thin Blue Line;
The women and children in the Legion of the Brave;
And Susan Burdett.

'It is not the critic who counts; not the man who points out how the strong man stumbles, or where the doer of deeds could have done them better. The credit belongs to the man [or woman] who is actually in the arena, whose face is marred by dust and sweat and blood; who strives valiantly; who errs, who comes short again and again, because there is no effort without error and shortcoming; but who does actually strive to do the deeds; who knows great enthusiasms, the great devotions; who spends himself in a worthy cause; who at the best knows in the end the triumph of high achievement, and who at the worst, if he fails, at least fails while daring greatly, so that his place shall never be with those cold and timid souls who neither know victory nor defeat.'

Theodore Roosevelt
'The Man in the Arena' speech at the Sorbonne, Paris, France
23 April 1910

CONTENTS

INTRODUCTION:
HOW ONE SERIAL RAPIST
CHANGED NEW ZEALAND POLICING

IT WAS 1993, AND SOUTH Auckland was being terrorised by a serial rapist. As far as we, the police, knew then, he'd appeared suddenly in February that year in Manurewa, which was part of my police patch. Later we found out that he'd already been offending for ten years. The long trail of misery he left behind was enormous. His victims over the course of those years included 50 to 70 girls and women who were attacked in their homes. We called him 'the Ghost'. His oldest victim was 47, and his youngest just 10 years old. Many victims were under 17.

At the beginning of the hunt for the Ghost I was 41 years old and a detective sergeant. By then I had been investigating murders, rapes and robberies and arresting perpetrators for years in South Auckland, my lifelong patch. As this investigation dragged on, however, with the weeks turning into months and the offending happening over and over again, our inability to catch this particularly hideous criminal was gnawing at me.

Every new investigative initiative we tried met with yet another dead end. We struggled to get regular staff to prevent further rapes and violence and to investigate the crimes that had already been committed, due to the pressure of our policing area, a more general lack of staff, and what appeared to be little understanding of the sheer volume of the ongoing, brutal trail of carnage. Initially, the commitment to the task by the hierarchy was also questioned. When we did get a permanent team together, even then we still couldn't find this ghost prowling our streets. What would it take to catch this criminal?

After over a year and a half of fruitless searching, the management team for the operation began to understand that the way we were going about things needed to change. What we didn't realise at the time was that the system we would develop — off our own backs and with little help and no advice from the upper echelons of policing — would change policing of stranger rapes and murders in this country forever.

This was criminal profiling. Allied with scientific breakthroughs in identifying DNA left at crime scenes, along with novel computing systems, it gave us a tool for hunting and catching rapists and other violent offenders. We would build a 'profile' of the likely offender from a synthesis of his criminal past and his characteristic behaviour at a rape scene. By creating this profile from past behaviour, we could search for the offender in the present.

This change not only broke with policing convention and methodology at the time, but it would also alter the direction of the rest of my career.

FOLLOWING OUR SUCCESSFUL HUNT FOR the Ghost and, shortly afterwards, the Lone Wolf, I was one of the very small team setting up and operating the Criminal Profiling Unit. At the outset it had just three, sometimes two, members of staff, along with very important assistance from a computer guru and the scientists working with DNA at ESR (Environmental Science and Research). During my time there, between 1998 and 2007, we helped to resolve many of the stranger rapes in Auckland and around the country, both current and historical.

Although I'm not a great fan of statistics, the following example is interesting. The most rapes ever reported in one year in New Zealand was 1265 in 1993, the year we started Operation Park. The following year the number dropped to 509; the year after that, to 435. There may have been many factors that influenced these figures, as they always do with statistics, but however superficial they remain dramatic.

The homicides we attended around the country were generally high-profile cases. In some our squad was able to focus the inquiry; in others we had little influence one way or the other. Profiling is not a silver bullet that will influence the investigation process of all homicide inquiries, just an extremely useful tool, as this book will show.

Our work benefited from the use of two databases in particular — one which held the data of charged persons together with a coded offence type and their addresses at the time of being charged, and the other which held details of behavioural aspects of the crimes. The first was primarily used to generate geographic and criminal profiles that we used to create suspect lists, which were used to great effect in a number of investigations. The second helped us to link crime to crime, and crime to offender, through analysing similarities in (especially) rape behaviours.

The CPU that we set up back in 1998 is now known as the Behavioural Science Unit. It currently operates with a team of five: a detective senior sergeant in the role of supervisor, two registered psychologists and three intelligence staff who manage the behavioural database. In the wider police operation, sex squads work in all districts and include CIB (Criminal Investigation Branch) teams focused on either adult sexual assault or child protection. These groups are well resourced and ring-fenced from other operational work. There is a strong training programme around interviewing — a crucial part of any investigation — including advanced interviewing streams for suspects, adult victims and child victims. The child protection teams work out of multi-agency centres with wrap-around victim support and social worker teams. Specially trained staff interview all victims, with the interview recorded on video and using open-ended cognitive interview techniques. The attending police would have taken just a bare-bones preliminary notebook statement to guide the investigation until the all-important victim interview could take place.

Court practices have changed, too. Victims are assessed for vulnerability, and often their video interviews are played as their evidence. Some cross-examination may take place, but this is often done remotely via a video link so that the victim cannot see the accused and is sitting somewhere comfortable where they have support people. On occasions when victims are physically present in court, the old-school partitions are put up so they cannot see the accused and vice versa. Trials are now very victim-orientated; court services for victims (CSV) staff employed by the Ministry of Justice will manage the logistics of getting each victim up into the courtroom via a safe route.

PLAYING A ROLE in identifying, charging and convicting rapists meant we were taking a sociopathic and brutal person off the street for many years and preventing more innocent lives from being destroyed. The work felt very meaningful; it was satisfying to know that we were making a long-term difference to the safety of women and girls, as well as giving victims a measure of closure. The number of criminals who become or develop into serial rapists isn't high. The 30 or 40 rapists, including Joseph Thompson and Malcolm Rewa, whose cases we processed were responsible for a great percentage of all the stranger rapes. Some others we hadn't personally dealt with, but the details of their crimes were now in our databases. We could study their behaviour and know our enemy.

It was a time of great change, and I was fortunate (and proud) to be in the right place at this pivotal moment — and up for the challenge.

1. SURVIVING IN THE TRENCHES IN SOUTH AUCKLAND

MY FIRST YEARS ON THE street as a young police officer proved to be a steep learning curve. I went in hoping that we'd be making a big difference, but soon discovered that rather than aiming for any great achievements in putting the world to rights, ensuring my own survival was the first bridge I'd need to cross.

I started at the Ōtāhuhu police station in August 1971, aged nineteen, working in 'I-Cars' — incident cars, now known as first-response vehicles. Most of my cadet mates started in central Auckland, Wellington or Christchurch, where they probably spent their first year walking the beat. That would have been a less dramatic start compared with my own crash course. South Auckland was, and remains today, a hot-bed of crime at many levels. It would remain my patch for the rest of my career. There was very little station politics and even fewer big bosses. But despite having lived in the area since I was twelve years old, it still took a while to bed myself into the environment and the work.

The work was authentic, raw and exciting, with interesting staff and a high level of job satisfaction. Many found it dispiriting that no matter how many crimes we solved, how many car-theft rings, burglary teams or aggravated robbery teams we broke up, the crimes just kept happening and it seemed like we were having no effect at all. However, while we were catching these teams of villains we were keeping on top of it and keeping anarchy at bay. Plus, we were making a difference for the victims. This was really the point of our duty and service: to make a difference for the victims, whoever they were and wherever they came from. Our court system is set up to ensure that defendants get a fair trial, and there appear to be numerous defence solicitors who are simply working to get their client off — sometimes by dubious means. It seemed to me then (and still does now) that we, the police, were there to make sure the victim got a fair trial too. Sometimes it seemed we were the only ones trying to do this; it was clear to me early on that the truth is not as powerful a weapon in court as it should be. But it was the only one we had.

My initial impression during my first few weeks at Ōtāhuhu police station was that I had walked into a lunatic asylum where chaos prevailed. The violence from the streets did not always stop at the station door, leading to periods of bedlam. Raucous shouting and screaming, along with fighting, would continue inside the cell block with no relief, for no apparent reason. Excessive drinking and the aftermath of domestic violence were common causes. The watchhouse counter was also often chaotic, with friends and family of arrested people clamouring to be heard. Some of these folk ended up joining their friends in the cell block. Along with the blood on the floor and the drunkenness, there were also clearly issues of mental health affecting many among the wild throng.

After midnight, most of the violence and noise died down and the quieter night-shift hours took over. This time provided the odd, shall we say eccentric, older senior police officer with a chance to explain their plans for how we should be dealing with the 'scum' and 'scrotes' on the street. I remember one idea for which the proposer had even drawn up a plan of execution. It involved putting machine-gun posts on the motorway bridge between Ōtara and Papatoetoe. Were these policemen, I wondered, really part of the last bastion — the thin blue line — between the criminal and the civilised world? Or was it just an expression of bravado to pass the quieter hours? These few eccentric members were, luckily, more than compensated for by the sane officers who offered much-needed mentorship to younger police.

Our section senior sergeant Don McConnell was one such sane officer. He had been one of the country's very early cadets, so I guess he had some knowledge of what I was trying to adjust to and digest. This young (30 years old) yet calm, disciplined and respected senior sergeant played a big part in me surviving my first year in that confused, often violent and brutal, somewhat crazy place. Among the many lessons I learnt from Don was the skill of being in respected control without being distant or a bully. Don was clearly destined for a high-up role in the police. This destiny was not denied him — he was eventually made a superintendent and a district commander and was always held in high regard by staff.

I was not actually useful for a long time, but eventually I found my feet and became accustomed to being in public in a uniform and woken up to the real world of policing, South Auckland style. My work ranged from talking down suicidal teenagers only a couple of years younger than myself, to dealing with dead, mutilated and decomposing bodies. Some were only very recently dead from suicide — hanging, or a shotgun to the head. Others, mostly old folk, had been dead for weeks. All had their own distinctive smells and visual horrors. I learnt to deal with advising the next-of-kin, defusing domestic disputes, and handling brawls in public bars involving combatants twice my age and size.

I didn't have time to dwell on the reasons for all this chaos and death. It was a time when naivety vanished quickly and confronting the tragic reality of many people's lives became a daily experience. Right from the start I was surrounded by so much death that the sad truth is it began to seem first unremarkable, then unmemorable, and finally routine. I suspect it was a way of coping with the relentlessness and sobering reality of this world, but it made the lives of those whose deaths I was dealing with seem cheapened and unimportant. At the first deaths I attended I was conscious of the sadness of those left behind, and the lives that their loved ones had lived. But as time went on, due to the sheer volume of untimely deaths we processed and investigated, each corpse became just another dead body. I worried that I might become callous, heartless and unemotional; that each death would become just another job to be done.

I apologise now to those members of the public who had the misfortune, in their time of need, to have me turn up at their door during these first few vulnerable months I spent as an officer. Later, with time and with guidance from senior staff, who had, I am sure, experienced the same feeling, I managed to master the delicate art of being both efficient and compassionate. Later still, when I became one of those senior staff myself, I made sure I remembered what it had been like and would try to help younger police officers when they arrived.

IN THE 1970S Ōtāhuhu was a working-class suburb with three large freezing works, and the clientele of the public bars reflected this. There was little poetry, dreaming or pretence, only the confronting realities of life and death, raw and sobering and in my face. Rational conversation was never an option with drunks. My colleagues and I always had each other's backs, preventing the coward's punch or a flying bottle.

My first domestic call-out was in Ōtara. My companion on this job was a quiet constable who didn't seem to have an aggressive bone in his very lean body. He had only recently graduated so knew little more than me. On our arrival at the property, a ramshackle state-house bungalow surrounded by the double-storey state houses that dominated the landscape in Ōtara back then, there was no doubt in our minds that we were at the right place. We could hear the loud obscenities and other noises; it sounded like a war movie on television with the volume turned up. I clambered out of the car, with the lesson notes on Domestic Disputes that we'd learnt verbatim at Trentham resounding in my brain.

- Separate the parties.
- Talk through their issues calmly.
- Make a cup of tea.
- Call for a local vicar.
- Don't be judgemental.
- Prevent violence.
- Resolve their differences.
- Arrest if offence clearly committed.

Whoever wrote these lesson notes had clearly never attended a real domestic incident, and certainly not one in Ōtara. Naively, I had expected to be received by at least one of the parties in the house with some enthusiasm — perhaps even cordiality — but this was not the case. As we climbed out of the car, the neighbours were all hanging over the fences calling us 'pigs'. These onlookers fell into two categories. One group was shouting obscenities urging us to leave, while others encouraged us to enter the house to get smashed up, thereby increasing the violence content of the night's entertainment. Both groups were baying for blood — ours.

It was an ominous situation. I felt very alone; a feeling I soon learnt to become accustomed to. My heart was thumping as we reached the open door, where I immediately found the family mongrel. I learnt later that the dog at many such homes commonly sits under the house near the doorstep, where one of the wooden palings is missing, scratching its fleas and often with a new litter of flea-ridden pups. The local name of this particular breed was 'The Baird's Road Special', after the road that ran through Ōtara. Attracted by the flapping of my lower serge trouser leg, the creature latched itself to my ankle. Judging by the ferocity of its grip, I could tell it wouldn't be removed any time soon. But I had bigger concerns awaiting me.

The scene that greeted us was shambolic. A couple in their forties were shouting abuse and flinging bottles at each other. Copious amounts of blood was splattered around the kitchen walls and on the floor where the battle was taking place. I guessed there had been some physical contact, or one or more of the missiles had found its target. The kitchen was consistent with the outside of this run-down home. There was little in the way of furnishings or household contents apart from empty and half-full beer bottles in the kitchen sink, and more empty bottles and other rubbish scattered about the floor.

I glanced at my partner, hoping he would have some idea of what to do, but he looked equally lost. I figured that making a cup of tea wasn't going to happen, even if I had known where the kettle was. Anyway, boiling water would not have been a recommended addition to the present scene. A vicar seemed even more out of place in this environment, and in any case I had no idea what his phone number would be, even if I'd had a phone. It was obvious that sitting this pair down to talk through their problems was also unlikely to bring about a useful outcome. The couple had probably been married, or at least together, for longer than I had been alive, so any advice from me would be both inadequate and unlikely to be well received.

From their lack of response to, or even acknowledgement of, our arrival, it was clear that these two were well accustomed to police intervention in their brutal married life. There were no children about, which was a blessing. Unfortunately, this proved not to be the norm in many of the domestics I later attended.

The dog attached to my ankle seemed to become more energised by the smell of blood, continuing to grip my serge blue trousers tightly. Perhaps it was used to receiving a considerable kicking by this stage of proceedings, but I was still new to the game. I remember wondering whether it was the familiarity of the police serge trouser leg that she recognised as something to attack.

After what seemed like hours, but was probably only a minute or so of indecision and confusion, the brawl was brought to a sudden end with the arrival of dog handler Tony Whiteside. In an instant he and his dog Rick had the drunken male on the floor and in handcuffs.

Well, I thought, this guy knows what he's about, so I followed his lead. I'd barely taken a breath before we were back at our police car and were putting the male in the back seat. The woman had now turned her anger on to us and was fighting us in an attempt to keep her man at the address. Perhaps she needed a target for practising her beer-bottle-throwing accuracy.

Still relishing their night-time entertainment, the neighbours had become even more worked up. It was like the Romans at the Colosseum watching the Christians being eaten by lions. My ankle actually felt like it had been gnawed at by a lion. The abuse being yelled now fell into two categories again. One faction was calling us pigs and egging the loving couple on to 'Give the pigs the bash.' The other was now accusing us of overusing force as their struggling neighbour was shoved head-first into the back seat of the police car after first bouncing off the doorframe.

Far from being a knight in shining armour riding a white stallion and protecting an innocent maiden, everybody — from the prisoner, to the neighbours, to the assault victim, to the family dog — hated us. The real world of policing was turning out to be nothing like cadet training at Trentham had made out, and not at all what I had expected. A lesson in selfless duty and service despite provocation occurred right there and then. I did wonder, though, who had reported the domestic incident to the police, as nobody I encountered seemed either concerned or surprised about it.

Over the next year or so, I visited the same address many times. The lack of welcome was usually the same. I did, however, get the better of the dog, which I noticed went missing after a while. I wondered if it had attached itself to the wrong ankle at some point.

THE LESSON I learnt from attending this first domestic dispute was that, much of the time, we wouldn't get any thanks for carrying out our duty. We would simply move on to the next thankless task. After all, it was what we were being paid for, and what we had signed up for. We were told both at training and while out on the streets that most homicides were committed in exactly these situations. On a positive note, we must have prevented a few homicides over the years — or at least delayed them.

Many years later I read a note from a High Court judge after the very long serial rape trial of Malcolm Rewa (aka the Lone Wolf) in 1998, recorded later in this book. The judge presiding at the trial noted the often thankless task of duty and doing what was right and necessary. It was comforting to have such an esteemed member of the judiciary recognising this.

The feeling I'd had of being alone also needs some explanation, because of course it wasn't in fact the case. I believe we had — certainly in those days — most of the public supporting us and, of course, the rest of the police. It is hard to describe, but much later on a line from the war series *Band of Brothers* resonated with me: 'We stand alone together.' This sums up those feelings, which carried over into my relationships with associates outside of the police. I was working in a dangerous environment in which I had to surround myself with people I could trust. Whenever I was feeling my way and unsure of myself, I felt that the only people I could let my guard down with were other police officers. Relationships outside of this trusted group got terminated, or faded away, or became conducted at arm's length. This was certainly the case in my 'bedding-in' year.

One schoolmate of mine, with whom I'd worked factory night shifts as a teenager, was an avid cannabis smoker. I assumed that he thought I didn't know. At one point we'd talked about travelling the world together, but I decided to stick with the police. I heard from him years later, on his return to New Zealand — his plan then was to go up north and grow cannabis for a living. I never heard from him again. Our friendship just faded away.

As another example, it took a year or more to feel safe and easy with those in the likes of rugby teams who were living in the area I policed. This was all part of being a newbie policeman in my patch and not really knowing how to fit in without letting the police down. Many people were, of course, looking to trip me up and compromise my position. The easiest way to deal with that was to keep my distance and stand alone. I played in sports teams where I was the only policeman. To many, I probably seemed arrogant and aloof. This changed over time as I learnt how to stand alone while remaining within the community *without* coming across as a bit of a jerk.

Getting a feel for my place in the environment involved much more than getting used to being in uniform and the constant daily work of domestics, street disorder, car chases, sudden deaths, fatal motor accidents and attending court. I'd entered an unfamiliar world that I wasn't really part of — or so it felt at first. Of course the local police *were* part of the place, but it took time to feel as if I fitted in; at first it was a bit like being the Pope at a drug-fuelled heavy metal punk concert. However, I soon began to really enjoy this adventure and getting to grips with what was involved with policing in South Auckland. Many of the older staff I'd met on arrival came from a different policing style — i.e. give them a kick up the backside and lead them home by the ear to their parents to sort out. We were entering a different world, and while most moved with it, the odd one or two didn't. As it turned out, though, many of my fellow police officers were ones I could trust to help me survive in South Auckland in this changing world.

The people I dealt with in the course of my work came from many different social groups. I learnt early on that as far as most of them went, no one person was more credible than another. Shopkeepers and homeowners lied for insurance purposes. Lawyers lied to get their clients off. Teenagers lied because they felt like it. Criminals lied to beat a rap. Some lied because it was all they knew. Everyone lied to cover their backsides. When I heard or read some of the media reports on incidents I'd attended, they were so twisted that I wondered if they were reporting on some other event.

There were also local idioms I needed to understand. Not long out of training, we locked up a young gang prospect for robbing a young boy of his new shoes, leaving him sitting bruised and barefoot on the footpath. When I questioned the perpetrator, he said, 'Yeah, I spooned the egg.' This was apparently an admission, but I had no idea what it meant. Colleagues told me later that, in general terms, it meant he'd knocked over a white guy and robbed him. There was much more of this sort of stuff to learn.

The perpetrator of that robbery went on to become a senior gang member and has spent much of his life in prison. Clearly, my dealings with him had no good effect on his future. To be honest, caring about the long-term future of someone you'd arrested wasn't really in the job description at that time. Once I'd gained more experience, I realised I needed to try to make a difference for *everyone* — if I could. Sometimes, making that difference meant putting someone in prison for as long as possible.

NONE OF US looked forward to dealing with sudden deaths and serious or fatal motor accidents — which, in the early '70s, were the police's concern. The traffic department got to deal with the accidents that didn't involve injury.

The Southern Motorway was a death trap at any time, but particularly so after hotel closing time. Tip Top corner — where the ice-cream factory overlooks the motorway — was often an accident site, right on our boundary. I remember dark, rainy nights with flashing red lights on ambulances and fire engines, and the three overwhelming smells each fatal motor accident brought: alcohol, petrol and ruptured human viscera — the smell of death. That last is a smell like no other: putrid and pungent, yet different from rotting or burnt flesh. It was a smell that never left my uniform unless it was dry-cleaned. I have many unpleasant memories of those wet, sad nights with those dead and mangled young men and women, often very intoxicated, whose lives had ended in the mortuary after a night out.

While dealing with dead bodies became commonplace, the deaths of children were always extremely hard to cope with. Five years after I graduated from Trentham, the first of my six children was born. Once, after the trauma of pulling the body of a child the same age as my own two-year-old from the bottom of a swimming pool, along with his tricycle, I rushed home desperate to set eyes on my son. It was only after seeing him safe and well that I was able to return to work to complete the file for the coroner relating to the other young boy's death. I was only 24 or 25 at the time.

There was also the matter of accepting generational policing, which you dealt with when you joined the front line and then again — from the other side — when it was your time to retire and the new brigade was arriving. Some of the senior sergeants working at Ōtāhuhu in 1971 were 50 to 60 years old; at that time the compulsory police retirement age was 60. I was informed that the average age reached by police officers *after* retirement was 62.

This sobering stat — meaning that the average police officer could expect to live only two years following retirement — has never been satisfactorily explained. I presume that this low age at death was a result of a lifetime of the stress and trauma of police work coupled with a sudden change in lifestyle and the ceasing of shift work.

These older police officers were from a completely different world to mine, but I still learnt a lot from them. I never judged them for any flaws they might have or any actions they might have carried out — most were great teachers of the practical basics and the little details that helped us survive on the job. It was clear, however, that a few had run their race. George was one such example.

He was a legendary figure because of his eccentric ways, many of which I witnessed first-hand. George had apparently fallen offside with the bosses on many occasions — I was advised to ask his advice if I ever got into trouble, as he had enjoyed a very successful career of winning fights with the hierarchy. At that time the police had a large black book containing a multitude of regulations; George reportedly knew the book inside out. Regulation 46 listed the many ways a police officer could get into trouble without even trying.

Despite nearing the end of his career in the police, George was still a senior sergeant on night shift every five weeks. It was a wicked shift regime of night shifts, early shifts and late shifts that we all suffered under; it went against the best medical advice, even back then. Those non-police workers who were on permanent night shift were apparently on a better regime than us.

The older you were, the harder these shift rosters became. Naturally, George struggled with it as he neared retirement. But, typical George, he manoeuvred around it in his own eccentric way.

At Ōtāhuhu, night shift was 11 p.m. to 7 a.m. but line-up — where batons, notebooks, handcuffs and dress code were checked, usually by the sergeant — took place at 10.45 p.m. After line-up we armed ourselves with the stolen car list hot off the teleprinter, along with any outstanding jobs, before hitting the streets. Many senior sergeants also supervised this line-up ritual, but in my experience George rarely did.

He would come in for duty wearing a greatcoat and carrying his slippers. On night shift he was responsible for the station, including the watchhouse and any prisoners, and for supervising any major incident that arose during his shift. After checking the prisoners, he had to clear the correspondence from the in-tray on his desk. He would also make sure there were no inspectors marauding south from Auckland Central, which could happen at any time but especially early in the night shift. Any surprise visit by one of these commissioned officers was referred to as a 'shark in the harbour' or 'shark in the park', depending on where you came from. The call would go out over the police radio to warn all staff of the officer in our midst. This term was popularised in the name of a local police television show in the late '80s and early '90s called *Shark in the Park*.

George took a quick five minutes to check the cells and another twenty minutes to empty his in-tray, which he did by sending any files on suspects to Invercargill, at the other end of the country, where there was a new freezing works. This was in response to every station in New Zealand sending their files to Ōtāhuhu for years because the suspect was 'believed' to be working at one of our three large freezing works. These suspect files would float about the country in an alternative universe destined never to be resolved. George used a fountain pen with light blue ink and his scrawl was enormous — half a dozen words would fill an A4 page. He would usually be eating an orange when he arrived and there would frequently be drops of orange in among the blue ink. In any event, the out-tray was quickly filled and the in-tray just as quickly emptied.

George would then take a large, 6-inch nail and hammer the sliding door between the watchhouse and the operations room closed; partly because it let a draught through and partly as a reminder to the watchhouse keeper not to disturb him unless it was an emergency. Then he would pull his greatcoat up over himself, slide his feet into his slippers and turn the lights out in the operations room, which opened off the area containing the senior sergeant's desk. The telephonists' room next to his desk was unmanned on night shift. George was clearly immune to sleep disturbance from the phones, radio calls at the operations desk, or the loud and irritating sound of the teleprinter printing off lists of stolen cars and messages from around the country.

This meant that all incoming calls to the station came directly to the operations room, which was manned by one constable. As George had turned the lights out, this constable had to work by torchlight, answering phones, writing down incoming jobs and directing patrol vehicles. It was like something out of a *Carry On* movie.

This awkward task became mine on occasion. One night, my completing a 180-degree turn in a new patrol car in pursuit of a suspicious vehicle was, unfortunately, witnessed by a visiting shark in the harbour from Auckland. This resulted in me being grounded for a month on night-shift operations — including a week with George.

The early-shift senior sergeant would arrive sometime before

7 a.m. to find an empty in-tray and prisoners well checked by George. George would also check the night's occurrences so he could brief the incoming senior sergeant before wandering his merry way home. Of course, if anything went awry at any time during the shift, George was available to deal with it. His extensive experience meant that he did so efficiently and without any fanfare or panic, even if he was half asleep.

George was finally promoted to a commissioned officer just before he retired. This gave him insufficient time to cause much trouble among the upstairs-office dwellers.

Other senior sergeants, while perhaps not as eccentric as George, had their own ways of dealing with the problems of the day or night. They were the source of much amusement and wonder to us younger police staff, but our generation lost much with their passing: their common sense, and their sense of justice. While some were more inclined to use the older methods of policing, they were still great mentors, teaching calmness, fairness and how to adapt to a policing world. It was clearer and cleaner in the front line than in the political world that existed up there in the clouds — a world we newbies knew nothing of but some of the senior staff did. It was very easy to get kicked out of the job in those early vulnerable months and years, and these senior sergeants protected us from that. Even if they sometimes seemed a little tough, we young ones knew where we stood with them — as did the criminals. These older police staff never left us without a clear message or direction — even if it was perhaps a little old-fashioned at times.

MY FIRST INVOLVEMENT with a serious crime was when a near-dead man was found in his car at the Panmure Basin car park. We were later told that he had received seventeen stab wounds to the neck. Somehow, despite being elderly, he survived the ordeal! This whodunit crime was a big deal in the early '70s. All South Auckland police staff and many Central staff on late and night shift were at or near the scene, which was cloaked in thick fog. Keith Allison and I were in the only car in South Auckland not at the scene. But finally we were also called in, to bring some petty item required by the Criminal Investigation Branch (CIB). Unfortunately, I was driving, and stopped right next to the car where the near-deceased man had been found.

District Commander Chook Taylor, Detective Inspector Hutton and many CIB and uniformed NCOs were all there, looking very important and staring directly through the fog at the driver of the grey Holden parked in the middle of their crime scene. The message was clear — move — but, as was often the case with the old 1969 Holdens, the gears became stuck. I had to get out of the car, stoop under the bonnet and bash the gearbox casing. Hearing uncomplimentary comments coming from the ensemble, I moved away from the scene as quickly as I could. The fog was so thick that they probably couldn't have identified me. The CIB and the district commander tended to be somewhat aloof from us foot soldiers back then, so wouldn't have known me anyway. Times change, and by the time I joined CIB later that decade, the aloof members of the police were integrated into the service, at least in South Auckland.

The offenders who'd attacked the elderly man were quickly arrested due to an old practice that flourished at the time in patches like Panmure, Papakura and Pukekohe, and every small town in New Zealand. The local senior sergeant or sergeant would go through the pubs with his staff before closing time, to see who was about. I'm sure this practice still takes place in many areas where the local pub is the gathering place for those who are likely to commit some villainy after closing hours and where the brawls are likely to occur. Back then, the senior sergeant in Panmure was the legendary Ross Dallow — and he had sighted the two offenders drinking with the victim a few hours earlier on just such a pub visit.

We policed the world, or our patch of it, with what we had available, what was in front of us, and with the systems that worked at that time.

2. STARTING OUT

IT'S SAID THAT IF YOU want to find what you are looking for, you must follow your footprints to where you've come from. Your DNA mix might provide the ingredients of the cake, but how it's mixed and cooked, by the people who influence the road you take, is reflected in how you live your life.

My parents worked dairy farms, as did their parents before them. All my parents, uncles and aunties went to a small village school in Turua, a small town on the Hauraki Plains, as did my generation. I have a photograph of the school in around 1920, with them all there outside the old school building where I started in the primers nearly 40 years later. Their generation's input into the area seems greater than any efforts since then. Although life was harsh and sometimes brutal for them, it was also somehow simpler. They were harder and more resilient than the generations that followed and their expectations were much lower. Neither of my parents went to high school.

My maternal grandmother got scalped in 1924 when her long hair became caught in the milking machine. The nearest hospital was in Thames, to the north across the Waihou River, and the Kopu Bridge would not be completed for another four years — this meant a slow boat trip to Thames to obtain medical attention from the local doctor, Dr Bathgate. He recorded the incident in his 1972 book *Doctor in the Sticks*, recalling that she was (understandably) in a state of shock when she arrived, her scalp quite bare. He must have been a skilled doctor, because after a number of skin grafts she was finally able to return home, wearing a wig and looking perfectly normal.

My grandmother died in the early 1960s, but it was well after this that I was told about this accident and learnt that she wore a wig. The pages containing the information about her had been torn out of the family copy of *Doctor in the Sticks*. It seemed that hard times were not just moved past, but treated as if they'd never happened. Another family story came into sharp relief much later, when I was a serving police officer. In 1874, a great aunty on my father's side of the family was kidnapped at the age of eight by Māori in Taranaki. The kidnapping was an act of revenge against her father who had cleared land in an area that the local Māori held sacred. Many had been killed there years earlier in a skirmish during the Land Wars.

After years of searching, including following up sightings in North Auckland, Caroline (Queenie) Perrot was recognised around 50 years after her kidnapping by a niece in Whakatāne. Apparently she was the spitting image of her mother at the same age. Queenie had no memory of her first eight years of life. She chose to remain with her Māori family. I'm guessing that this memory loss was dissociative amnesia as a result of her early trauma. I have witnessed examples of this condition many times as a police officer dealing with victims of crime.

FOR ME — like everyone, I imagine — memories from over 60 years ago are like a broken old movie in which an arrangement of small fragments assemble themselves as if I was gazing into a kaleidoscope. Even then, I cannot be sure if it's a real memory as opposed to one created by photographs or stories related to me by older relatives. I know this from police investigations involving false memories, and from the unreliability of witnesses, even eyewitnesses. I know how dangerous it can be to be 100 per cent sure of your memories — especially old ones. Bearing this caveat in mind, I apologise to anyone who may have a different recollection of the events I report in this book.

I was the youngest of eight children and very much at the tail end, by some margin — 'the little chicken'. My mother was 42 years old when I was born, on St Valentine's Day 1952, so I must have been a shock to my parents and probably to the rest of the family, given that my eldest sister was sixteen. An earlier family photograph with all seven children minus me reflected this. It remains a constant reminder on the wall at the Hauraki Road home. I was an afterthought, a postscript.

Turua is a village of a few hundred people on the banks of the Waihou River — a very tame, uneventful and predictable place, but one that gave us children the freedom to venture out on to the river and further afield. It was a place where everyone knew everyone else. Decades later, I can still name all the kids in my class from primer one onwards. This strange, protected environment — which now seems so primitive — reflected a simple lifestyle, with stability being the defining word to describe my family environment. Simplicity, but with a sense of belonging, was the key to producing a solid foundation. Just how important that is I was to find out many years later, when I was analysing the behaviour of some individuals who had been given an altogether different start in life. I feel now that I have little real connection to my earlier life, but of course I do and I owe much to it.

In this protected environment, though, much of the outside world was kept from us children, leaving us in blissful ignorance. From the adults around me I assimilated the view that the freezing workers and wharfies in the cities were lazy folk who held the country to ransom and lived off the hard work of the farming community, who made up most of the honest and decent people in the whole country. This was not that long after the Auckland wharfie strikes of 1951. Obviously, these happenings were a bit raw for the farmers entrenched in the swamp. But little nuances and prejudices such as these do sneak into the make-up of your inner self. Later, as a police officer, these learnt prejudices were reawakened when I was involved in the numerous search warrant operations relating to mass thefts from both the freezing works in Ōtāhuhu and the wharves. However, I did begin to learn that it was a mistake to generalise — of course not all wharfies and freezing workers were thieves and layabouts, but it would take much personal experience and knowledge to iron out these early preconceptions.

I was mostly brought up by my mother; I don't recall ever having a conversation with my father. At that stage, apparently, neither did my older brothers; though earlier my older siblings had known a different father. He had accompanied them everywhere, had been involved in community activities, Bible class outings and school events. They described him as a happy, whistling man when they were young children. Clearly I had arrived too late to see the happier side of this good man. Over the years I have thought a lot about why he was so taciturn later in life. He wasn't a war veteran, so that doesn't explain it. Friends I grew up with in our farming community report that their fathers were the same — not talkative. Perhaps he was just worn down with life and hard work on the farm by the time I was born.

Our family farm, situated not much above sea level, was originally a kahikatea swamp. Farms like these require very deep drains to make the drainage good enough to allow grass to grow. Rushes flourish in wet ground. If not kept under control, they tend to proliferate at scale and speed to cover the land. In my father's day, rushes were cleared and drains dug by shovel; nowadays it's done using machinery. The rushes on our farm had, despite the efforts of Dad and his shovel, spread out of control. He had been digging them out from a very young age, and was eventually defeated by them. He gave up on the farm, leaving a half-filled trailer along with his shovel in the centre paddock; a memorial to his defeat. It was a memorial I was reminded of every time I brought the cows in for milking from that centre paddock. Our farm dog learnt to jump a metre into the air to locate any cows hiding among the rushes, which had by then become a forest.

In the Christmas holidays we were packed up and sent to 2 Morrin Street, Ellerslie, to stay with my maternal grandmother (the one with the secret wig) and my Aunty Agnes, who had remained single. I figured this was so she was available to take my brothers, cousins and myself on trips to a fantasy world — the city of Auckland. Such a wondrous place — picnics on One Tree Hill, rides on the Devonport ferry, the zoo, the museum, trams, trolleys, buses and trains. And the movies on Queen Street, especially those at the Civic, with its stars and lions with red eyes.

Given the excitement generated by my Auckland holidays it was clear that I was not going to become a farmer and remain in Turua. But my family didn't remain there either. I had just turned twelve when we left the farm, in 1964, and moved to Papatoetoe, South Auckland. Dad just walked around the corner from our new home and got himself a job at the Bremworth carpet factory; Mum became the tea lady. Plenty of work in the 1960s.

WITH MEMORIES OF my holidays in Auckland vivid in my mind, I thought all my dreams had come true. However, living in suburban South Auckland was not at all what I'd expected.

I was a shy, nervy kid who had left a school of about 120 pupils, all from similar backgrounds, and all of whom I knew and whose families all knew ours. I'd attended that school from playcentre to Form Two. From this stable, safe, secure environment and its sheltered ignorance, I stumbled into the playground at Ōtara Intermediate School with a roll of over 1000 kids. Some of them had parents who worked in the freezing works or on the wharves. Influenced by what I'd overheard at home and in our farming community, I was wary of them. Having no knowledge of the way people lived in the city meant a quick learning curve when my lunch was stolen just minutes after I climbed on to the school bus on my first day. We live to learn how to survive.

In retrospect, Papatoetoe High School (which followed Ōtara Intermediate) was highly regarded during the '60s — although at one point, some disillusioned pupil burned down the gymnasium and the woodwork room. One artistic wit played on this by drawing a picture of the offender carrying a lighted torch from the gymnasium to the woodwork rooms. The school's motto, *Digne Lampada Tradas*, means 'Be worthy to carry the torch'.

At high school I could get on with whatever I wanted without much disruption. There were fights in the school grounds, but they involved only those who wanted to be involved and were avoided by most of us. Some of the combatants in these schoolyard fights would cross my tracks later in my police work. Usually they ended up in the cells; the beginning often predicts the end.

Despite Papatoetoe being a middle-class suburb during the '60s, and home to many fine families, it also produced some notorious criminal families. Others in the community became their victims. In subsequent years I met many people representing both groups. Although I played sport with at least a few of those who later became notorious in villainy, clearly my antennae were not finely tuned back then. Looking back, I must have been in a deep sleep because the thieving, thuggery and general criminality would have been already in place and established with these boys by the time they were in their teens.

My academic work was average at best; I had little interest in it. 'Could do better' summed things up. The hypotenuse of a triangle was about as interesting to me as a hippopotamus's backside. Consequently, my exam marks were also only average, especially in maths. We used a grey book full of logarithms. To this day I have no idea what logarithms are. How I ever passed School Certificate maths is a mystery to me. I put it down to a dash of luck and a friendly marker.

I had no idea what I was going to do when I left school, but I did know what I *didn't* want to do. Factories were out of the question. A mate of mine and I had skipped off after school on Fridays to work for a firm called Dirty Work Tacklers, who hired out casual workers to factories over several night shifts. Although we were only sixteen we signed on as being over eighteen years, but I'm sure they didn't really believe us, being two skinny, young-looking Pākehā kids. The factory work was abysmal but the money was good. I also worked two months at the Bremworth carpet factory on night shift just after leaving school. The only staff members under 30 at the Bremworth factory were a big Māori guy called Bully and a skinny white guy who I called 'Gummy' because his teeth were rotten and falling out.

Bully and Gummy's conversation was a mystery to me, and I think sometimes it was a mystery to them as well. I met Bully again after finishing my police training. By this time he had given up working at Bremworth, latexing carpet strands together on permanent night shift, and become the leader of the local Black Power chapter. I never saw Gummy again, but thought he had probably died; he was the most sickly-looking young person I had ever known.

I got the idea to train as a policeman from an older schoolmate, Norm Reid, who had headed to police college himself. I had no connection with anyone in the police — I can find no record of any relative ever putting on the blue uniform — but the idea of 'good versus bad' was something I related to. It was a view largely formed by watching Western movies like *High Noon* and *Shane*, where good always prevailed. I was lucky to have a friend like Norm who influenced my decision, and we worked together briefly in Manurewa. Sadly, he died well before any man should.

To enter the police I was told I needed University Entrance accreditation. That meant I needed better grades. Being told this created a focus — and for the first time, I applied myself to my studies and did achieve that UE accreditation. Turned out, all I needed was a goal.

Biology was a favourite subject. In exams we were frequently asked to write an essay on deoxyribonucleic acid. This was a go-to question for me; little did I know that twenty-plus years later DNA would play a very important role in my life. I also recall a Sixth-Form English teacher helping me to learn a list of commonly misspelled words that I needed to know to pass the pre-entry test to join the police. I remember the words 'diarrhoea', 'haemoglobin' and 'haemophiliac' being on the list. I wish I had kept that list, as I am sure I have had to write all the words on it many times over in the past 50 years.

Having gained UE, this unprepared, naive and unsophisticated 'little chicken' headed off for a life in the police, starting with training college at Trentham in Wellington. Joining the police gave me a focus and a purpose. The work suited me fine for 50-odd years, offering something different around every corner. I am lucky indeed, and joining the police is something I have never regretted.

WE LEFT AUCKLAND Central Railway Station to commence our police cadetship in late January 1970, tumbling out at the Wellington Railway Station after a fourteen-hour overnight trip on what was then called the Limited. It was well named, the only breaks from a sleepless night being pies and cups of tea at a few towns along the route. Wellington Railway Station must have had the same architect as the one who drew up the plans for Auckland Railway Station, because at first I thought we had landed back where we started. But this impression was short-lived, lasting just until we'd met Senior Sergeant Croxford, the first of our police instructors. A solid, stern chap aged around 40, he was spotlessly turned out, with polished shoes and a red crown on the arm of his dark navy-blue serge uniform. There was no friendly smile or welcoming ceremonial verse to put us at ease. He was not well received by a nervous, excited group of pups who had not slept. A gruff, starchy man in an equally starched uniform was a little overwhelming and we went very quiet. As it turned out, we were well looked after and protected by all our instructors, and many still attend the police reunions we have every five years. I think the initial starchy reception was just to set the scene.

We met up with our equally quiet future inmates from the rest of the country in a place called Holland House. There we gained a little more insight into how we would be entertained over the next nineteen months. We were told clearly what was expected, and that we would not graduate unless we worked hard and obeyed the copious rules. From there we bused to the police training college at Trentham. We were in for a surprise when we pulled up on the parade ground. The shabby, grey corrugated-iron huts they called barracks had accommodated World War I soldiers before they headed to Gallipoli, and the World War II troops of the Second New Zealand Expeditionary Force had also trained there before leaving home, many forever. This would now be *our* home for the next nineteen months.

On sighting his new digs, one potential cadet didn't even get off the bus, instead turning around and heading straight back home. Wellington was referred to by everyone except the Wellingtonians as the 'Arsehole of New Zealand', and Trentham was '18 kilometres up it'— a view that was reinforced during the winter months when the place became frigid.

For the first eight months, the whole wing — about 80 of us

— were housed in two of these barracks, Huts 211 and 210 — furthest from the Training HQ, but next to the civilian apprentice barracks and the mess, or Luigi's as it was called. We were placed in cubicles containing a set of bunks and a single bed, accompanied by three sets of drawers and two wardrobes and a third wardrobe in the hallway — three cadets to each cubicle with a curtain to divide us from the rest. One 6- by 12-inch mirror on the wall and a solitary mat completed the total furniture included and, from memory, permitted; we would soon learn that the mat had a purpose other than comfort. The reality was that nothing more would have fitted into this cosy cubicle. Additional wall decorations were not permitted until we had got through our first eight months as junior cadets. We were to learn that we were at the bottom of the training college heap, below our instructors, the senior cadets, the recruits — even the police dogs. Senior cadets were the previous year's intake of seventeen-year-olds, who had been in the camp for a year by now; we were, obviously, the junior cadets. Recruits were older, nineteen years and upwards, and three wings of these went through Trentham each year on three-and-a-half-month courses.

Our first few nights included raids by the senior cadets. They had apparently spent the last term eagerly awaiting our arrival so they could exercise their ritual rights to attack us in the middle of the night and give us cold showers and cold baths filled with gun oil and goodness knows what else. After the first night's attack, we figured we would barricade and lock the barracks doors so they could not get at us, but after the familiar broom stick along the corrugated-iron walls, which would wake the dead and, like a siren during the Blitz, alert us to impending danger, we discovered that a couple of the seniors had hidden themselves in the roof. Like those within the Trojan horse, they fell down upon us and let the remaining horde in.

This friendly little welcome was of no great consequence and was soon over. We got on well with most of the senior cadets, both around the camp and on the sports fields where we joined forces against the remainder of Wellington and the Hutt. I suppose today it would be considered bullying, but it was actually just a slight distraction. No one left our wing because of it, and no one (that I was aware of) was seriously injured. And it was *nothing* compared with the real world we were to confront after training.

When we returned the favour to our junior cadets a year later, though, we were quickly stopped because over a dozen left in the first few weeks. This was considered to be partly due to our exhaustive physical welcome. And perhaps this was so, but more likely it was the impact of the environment as a whole that caused so many cadets of that particular wing to walk away. The prevailing view among the other trainees (and, I suspect, the instructors as well) was that if they couldn't survive a few cold showers, they'd have little chance on the cold streets they were training for. Regardless, from then on the tradition of night raids and cold baths for juniors was, I understand, curtailed or, at the very least, closely monitored.

Meanwhile a constant source of complaints by all of us and, apparently, every wing before and after us, was the poor standard of the food we received from Luigi's. Because of the frequent appearance of maggots in our meals, the refrain 'Maggots and flies, alive alive-o, alive alive-o' was commonly heard among cadets as we paraded and marched to our meals in full parade kit. Indeed, at one point the maggots became more common and fresher than usual. Previously we had to try to distinguish dead maggots from rice grains, but now the maggots were easy to identify. They were still moving. After yet another complaint it was discovered that a mouse (or several mice) had died above the kitchen servery's sliding windows and the maggots were dropping fresh on the meals as they were handed over. This was probably the only fresh meat we ever had there!

But we all survived, perhaps due to food parcels from home and perhaps due to the daily visits of an Indian man known as Mojo, who parked his blue-grey truck outside Luigi's at mealtimes. Using our small cash reserves — as cadets we were paid just $1200 a year, and most of us left Trentham with no money despite having arrived with some in the bank — we bought fresh fruit and nourishing food which sustained us through these times. I am embarrassed to record here that tricks were played on Mojo. These included locking him in his truck, jacking up his truck and removing a wheel, asking for yoghurt (which was the new fad) and when he'd stocked a lot of it, not buying any from him. Mojo persevered through all this and much more. I understand that many years later he owned half the real estate in Upper Hutt, bought off the backs of starving cadets and recruits at Trentham police training school. Good on him — and a personal thanks for hanging in there, despite the cruel tricks played on him by us and every wing before and after us.

THE INSTRUCTORS OFTEN tried to show us that they were in charge, which seemed to me wasn't something that needed to be proved. Commandant's parade and room inspections were central to this: white-glove checks for dust and the exact 12-inch fold-down of the sheet measured by ruler. The black blankets, placed neatly in the cupboard at the top of the wardrobe, had to be folded correctly with the red stripe exactly in the centre of the fold. If we got it right and looked at all smug about it, or the instructor had just got out on the wrong side of bed that day, we were required to roll under our bed or have the cubicle's mat rubbed down our perfectly clean and ironed serge uniforms, meticulously prepared for commandant's inspection, so that they picked up dust. Regardless of how well you swept the floor or the mat, the almost-black serge uniform would pick up some dust.

We had to have our spare uniform ready to change into for the commandant's parade five minutes later. If at parade this uniform was not perfect, with knife-edge creases in the trousers and boots polished to the point where you could see your face in them, cancelled weekend leave or the water tower beckoned. This water tower, near the Wi Tako (now Rimutaka) prison, looked down over Trentham camp. As punishment, we would have to run to the water tower carrying a chair, climb on the chair and wave to the instructor down on the parade ground. Alternatively, you could be ridiculed by having the whole section face punishment for your error, which usually meant everyone being confined to barracks over the weekend.

The strict discipline was, in fact, preparation for a career in the police, which is a disciplined service. Some of our group did not appreciate this at first, but we all settled into the routine. Our training might have been very strict, but it resulted in us learning self-discipline. If, out in the real world of policing, we refused to be told what to do and responded with childish rebellion to every order we received, we would put those around us in danger and chaos would ensue. You will find very few retired police officers who have anything but glowing reports of their time spent training at Trentham.

I do believe that once we settled in, most of us enjoyed our time at Trentham barracks. We were all in it together, and I suspect this led to the camaraderie that continues to this day. It was a watershed, perhaps even a metamorphosis, for many of us in different ways. It certainly was for me.

We were given a good grounding in the law, which was learnt verbatim, as well as some practical lessons — much of which I found to be of little use afterwards in the real world of policing. For some of the lads, the academic requirements were steep. There were tests most Saturday mornings. A few fell by the wayside after failing to pass. Others either left of their own free will or after getting into strife during the course. We started with around 82 cadets and finished with about 72.

At the time I was there, Trentham was a male domain. There were no female cadets, and most of the recruit wings who went through every three and a half months had very few female trainees among them. Recruit wings usually consisted of up to a hundred members, of which women never made up more than 10 per cent. The remainder of Trentham was an army establishment and I saw few females in their ranks, either. Consequently, female company was keenly sought after outside the camp domain.

The few female recruits who went through Trentham at the same time as me were housed at the end of the Headquarters building, which was surrounded by a white picket fence. We were advised that any cadet or male recruit seen to jump this fence would be instantly dismissed.

Of the 80-odd members in our cadet wing there were only about three or four with any Māori whakapapa. From the '80s onwards, the number of women, Māori and Pasifika recruits has, fortunately, increased. In recent years there has also been an enormous increase in Asian and Indian recruits, representing the change in the diverse population of the country.

After the new Police College was opened in 1981, the strict discipline dropped away to the extent that females and males shared accommodation, the military-style training of Trentham disappeared, and I hear the meals are now first-rate. The world moves on, and the Trentham police barracks have physically disappeared altogether. But they remain a special place for thousands of police trainees who went through this memorable, if tough, finishing school.

IN OUR FINAL MONTHS of training we went out on what was called Station Duty. We had no police authority, but accompanied sworn staff on their various duties. I particularly remember having to stand outside pubs when they were emptied out at 10 p.m. This was because we were not only unsworn but also underage, and therefore not allowed to enter licensed premises.

The drunks would be herded out past us kiddie cops. I think they saw us as part of the evening's entertainment. They enjoyed a verbal discharge of insults and what they seemed to think were original humorous remarks. 'Not old enough to go into a pub, eh sonny?' 'I'm the one you're after, Mr Policeman.' And, from the transvestites: 'Come with me, I'll teach you a thing or two, sweetie.' But even as new as we were, we had all heard these comments many times before.

Due to alcohol, I nearly ended up being an early leaver from training. In the third term, on a boring Saturday afternoon between sport seasons, a fellow cadet and I decided to purchase some beer at the local pub, the Totara Lodge. Unfortunately, just as we left with our half-dozen bottles of beer we were met by one of the recruit instructors. Our actions were of course illegal, as we were both underage (the drinking age being twenty at the time). This recruit instructor, known as Tex, gave us a wink as we left. We figured he was a cool guy and returned to barracks assuming that we had just dodged a bullet.

However, as is often the case, youthful optimism was followed by a kick up the backside. On Monday morning we were marched to Senior Sergeant Mick Tarling's office on a charge. We pleaded guilty to purchasing liquor underage and taking liquor into the barracks, and were fined ten dollars on each charge. This might seem trifling, but at the time it was equivalent to about two months' savings. But we weren't thrown out.

The guy I was with was Ted Cox, a top rugby player and cricketer. We suspected that the commandant, Teddy Hotham, viewed Ted as potentially his first cadet All Black in the making. Mick Tarling was the senior rugby coach. Had I been caught with anyone else, I think I would have had a return journey to Auckland on that very slow Limited, minus my uniform — but thanks (I believe) to Ted's sporting prowess I didn't have to find another occupation for the next 50-odd years.

As for the 'liquor in barracks' charge, I've always thought that was a bit unnecessary because the ceiling was full of empty beer bottles. One day the roof collapsed under the weight of them. But Ted and I didn't argue the charge; we were just relieved to have clung on to our cadet berets and be allowed to complete the course.

Graduation day was a sad event. I was still unsophisticated, naive and unprepared, but bolstered by the knowledge there were at least 70 other young guys in the same boat. During those past nineteen months I had gained confidence in the knowledge that while many of those around me had excelled at school, I was just as good as they were if I bothered to try, and better than most —

at least in the examination room. Many shared the same doubts and insecurity as I did, which resulted in an overall increase in confidence for each of us.

I managed to sneak into the top ten of the wing, though this placing didn't mean much in terms of our future in the job. Some were career-orientated, while others had different visions of their future within the police. I came ninth and Ted Cox came tenth. I retired as a detective sergeant and Ted as a detective superintendent, which proves my point. A few who beat both of us never went past constable or detective and were happy with that, and many who graduated well below us became commissioned officers.

In August 1971 we all left Trentham and dispersed to different parts of the country to start our careers as real policemen — still green and with no real idea of what to expect other than a few clues gleaned on Station Duty and a brain filled with lesson notes learnt verbatim. What we'd mostly learnt related to police culture. Foremost in this culture were values such as duty, service and honesty. These, along with the camaraderie that lives on, were the principal messages I took from my nineteen months at Trentham. There was also an appreciation of the excellent reputation gained by those who had gone before us — a reputation we had to live up to and maintain.

3. PAPAKURA — MY LONG-TERM PATCH

IN JANUARY 1973, AFTER EIGHTEEN months at Ōtāhuhu, I was transferred — along with many other police staff — about 20 kilometres south to Papakura. The Papakura station was in the process of being upgraded, but for now we all still worked from the small, quaint, but outdated little wooden police station. It had a couple of wooden cells, similar to dog boxes, out the back, plus a holding cell with a glass window.

Papakura became my patch for the majority of the next 25 years. Three of my fellow Trentham junior cadets, including Russell Lamb, also transferred to Papakura and a senior cadet, Ray Smith, was already there. Russell and Ray became my regular workmates in the trenches of South Auckland over the next 45 years — in the uniformed branch, in CIB, and in my later non-sworn role. Ray had many nicknames, but his original cadet's nickname was 'Spud', as he had come from Pukekohe, where they grew potatoes. Russell

Lamb has always been known as 'Lambo'.

The boss at Papakura was the late Mick Huggard, who ruled the town fairly — and with force where necessary. Mick lived in the police house next to the old station and the old courthouse, both of which fronted on to the main street. He could often be seen striding down the main street in his pyjamas and dressing gown to sort out disorderly idiots who were keeping him awake. They were usually to be found outside either of the two pubs and, on occasion, the Corvetto takeaway, which was directly across the street from his house. This was referred to by staff as Mick working his secondary job as a street cleaner. Resistance was not a recommended response. Mick was a large man with an equally robust reputation gained on the streets of Papakura and around the country. He was, apparently, banned from demonstrations after leading a baton charge at anti-Vietnam War demonstrators in Auckland during the visit of US Vice President Agnew in 1970. He was also, though, awarded a gallantry medal for disarming an armed offender in Wellington after he had left Papakura.

Mick was a character much loved by police and Papakura residents alike, while other senior staff were the go-to men with regard to many local troublemakers and army contacts. Papakura had a very large army presence. Although they mostly looked after their own, there were occasions when the army came into conflict with locals. We had the SAS boys, some very large Fijian army boys, and the local hardcore that every town has.

Everything ran smoothly at the station, with the senior staff guiding the younger staff and without internal politics interfering with our work on the street. The old policing style was still operating here. When there was trouble about town, Mick and other senior staff would simply ring up those involved and they would trot down to the station without a fuss. If they were fined, they'd be escorted over to the court to pay. Or, if they refused to pay, they'd take a holiday in prison for a month instead.

MY NEXT FEW years at Papakura station were exciting times. Car chases on night shift would sometimes follow stolen cars for 100 kilometres. The only other vehicles on the roads after 1 a.m., when most of these chases occurred, were the milkman and the bread-man who waved us by. By the end of these car chases there would often be over half a dozen police cars and the inevitable dog wagon. Many chases ended in crashes with the stolen car being damaged, but I cannot recall any injuries arising directly from a car chase. Regardless of requests from our bosses to cease the chases, they never stopped. For some reason the police radios always became ineffective at the same time as the request was broadcast. There were a lot of radio dead zones in our backyard.

At the end of a car chase, any offenders who foolishly tried to run from the scene would receive a few stitches in the backside after the attentions of an over-enthusiastic police dog. Many of the offenders were young so this was an early lesson, but one which some recalcitrant youths never learnt from and probably wore as a badge honouring the chase. Others learnt the lesson that every bad act has a consequence and didn't run the next time.

There were many pub brawls that resulted in much blood being spilt on the footpath. The dog section with Tony Whiteside and his colleagues, which covered South Auckland and also supported Central's dog section, was a most welcome sight when the dust was flying. The level of disorder at the hotels throughout Auckland led to a top-of-the-cliff policing initiative credited to then Assistant

Commissioner and Auckland Regional Commander Gideon Tait. He assembled a group of around twenty trained officers to address the problem. These officers had a paddy wagon and a dog attachment. They went through the hotels before closing time and locked up any intoxicated troublemakers to prevent some of the brawls, as well as sorting out any brawls that did occur. The impacts of this task force started to be felt in the mid-1970s as the number of pub brawls decreased. Some people were critical of the task force because many people arrested in pubs for drunkenness were perhaps only moderately intoxicated. However, the object was to identify troublemakers early, to remove them and therefore prevent the inevitable brawls starting.

When you debate a new idea or concept, the most relevant points are whether or not it worked and if there were any long-term issues arising from it. The task force did work, and the long-term result was a major drop-off in street warfare exploding out from the large pubs. The contrary view is, of course, that it infringed on personal freedom and rights, and pushed the boundaries of the law of the day.

From 1974 to 1975 I worked at the Manurewa Enquiry Office; Manurewa was the northern point of the Papakura area and bordering the Ōtāhuhu area. I was now learning to investigate the many series of burglaries and car thefts, hunt down the offenders and prepare the large prosecution files for court. This was more of a planned hunt than the reactive work of I-Car shifts. It also meant getting out of the punishing early/late/night-shift roster for the first time. In the Enquiry Office we worked five-day rosters of early (7 a.m. to 3 p.m.) and late (3 p.m. to 11 p.m.) shifts, including weekends. It was here that I learnt to investigate crime and the 'art of the hunt'.

In Manurewa at that time there was never any let-up on burglaries, stolen vehicles and other crime. In the '70s (and possibly also in the '80s), all burglaries, thefts, assaults, warrants, summonses, neighbourly disputes — basically everything — in Manurewa were reported to the police station or attended by one or more I-Cars, then put through to the Enquiry Office in the area concerned.

Most burglaries were committed by groups of youths aged ten to seventeen years. At one point the volume of burglaries became so extensive that we joined up with truancy officers and CIB to try to curb the problem. Brian from CIB joined me one day with a well-known young suspect, complete with long blond hair. We drove around the town while the suspect pointed out a few houses he had burgled. His memory was clearly giving him problems, as he conveniently forgot one house we already knew he'd burgled. Brian, not known for his patience, swung around from the front seat and grabbed the boy by his hair — which came away in Brian's hand. Our suspect was wearing a blond wig, that I hadn't clocked, but this worked out well for us because Brian had just uncovered the piece of evidence we needed. The wig had come from the very house burglary the boy had denied committing. How, I wondered, did this clever CIB guy know he was wearing a wig? I made a mental note to join CIB one day and key into this well of instinctive knowledge.

IN A VERY spread-out city like Auckland, with its very mobile criminal element, it was well accepted within the police that local crime was not always carried out by local criminals. Burglars from many diverse parts of Auckland would visit South Auckland to commit crimes, including burglary and the odd robbery. This also worked in reverse, of course. Our local South Auckland bad boys and girls would travel Auckland-wide to display their moral code of indifference to the person and property of others. The concept was obvious: the offenders would not be known in the area, and would also take their stolen goods back to another part of the city to dispose of. As most such crimes were committed in stolen cars, why would they do it in their own backyard when they could grab a free set of wheels to do it somewhere else?

The disadvantage to this approach was that the criminals did not know the area they were 'working' in as well as they did their own suburb. One such visitor to Manurewa in the 1980s came from a notorious family of robbers, burglars and drug dealers from Glen Innes, who had decided to commit an armed robbery in Manurewa in a stolen vehicle. He parked his getaway car facing home before walking across the road to a local jewellery shop, which he successfully robbed at gunpoint. Returning to where his getaway car was parked, he found to his amazement that a local car thief had stolen it in the few minutes he was away.

The result was that he had to run off down the road, on foot, with his loot and his gun, making him an easy catch for the local police. When caught, the offender commented that we should get on top of the car-thieving problem in our patch — it was embarrassing for out-of-towners. I doubt he ever returned to deep South Auckland to commit any further robberies after he was released from Mt Eden prison a few years later.

I got to know most of the most prolific offenders in Manurewa. Some grew up and settled down, but others just kept on their criminal path. We knew that if they were still committing burglaries, thuggery and general thieving when heading towards their thirties, they would probably be in trouble for the rest of their lives and, consequently, waste part of their lives in prison.

Two such recidivist young offenders who went on to become career criminals were the 'Jose twins', twin brothers who grew up in Manurewa. They both had Jose as their second Christian name and facially looked very similar; less so otherwise physically or behaviourally. One was scrawny, cocky and willing to take on any challenge without a second thought. The other was well-built, and more cagey and guarded. He had a reputation about town for being physical and was loosely tied to the drug scene, which probably led to his more circumspect approach to criminality. But the two stuck closely together. I arrested them many times over the years, starting when they were about sixteen years old and I was only 21. The arrests were mainly for burglaries, fraud and assaults, and at least one was on their birthday.

We regularly bumped into each other in the street. With great humour, they made no attempt to try to take a different road from the dishonest one they were on. They made no apologies for this either, accepting that being arrested, spending time in borstal and, later, prison, was just part of their chosen lifestyle.

Most times I locked them up, we shared some humorous anecdote together as I took their fingerprints. I'm not sure if this sort of familiarity is to be recommended; I doubt it would happen today. Back then, though, it seemed inevitable to me that tomorrow they would be back offending, with no remorse or thought of changing their ways — so why bother to make the arrest a bad experience for either of us? Besides, I was also learning the ways of criminals and how they lived, thought and operated. This was an interesting and useful experience, and would continue for many more years. Our job description in those days was to locate and lock up offenders;

it did not include social work. In previous years I guess they would have received a whack around the ear and a kick up the backside from some old-time officer. That system didn't seem to work now, as there were more young burglars than ever, but my methodology of friendly interaction and humorous exchanges clearly didn't work either. The Jose twins continued to burgle and steal for many years.

On one occasion I had dealt with Big Jose over a burglary and was out looking for Little Jose for the same burglary. I found them both near Wiri Mountain, wandering along the road. Both got in the car, Big Jose in the front seat and Little Jose in the back. Of course I'd already charged Big Jose, so he just came along for the ride. As we talked, I noticed that Little Jose kept on muttering a lot of nonsense in the back seat. Big Jose might have known what the problem was but there was no way he would enlighten me — as the bond between these two was greater than any I'd experienced between the staunchest gang members.

When we reached the station and went in, Little Jose collapsed at the watchhouse counter. Clearly something was wrong, so the watchhouse keeper, who happened to be Ray 'Spud' Smith, rang for an ambulance and we rushed Little Jose to hospital. We managed to find out from a worried Big Jose that when they had been up Wiri Mountain, his brother had crushed up some datura flowers and drank the liquid. This flower is a known hallucinogenic; it's also very dangerous and life-threatening. This info was passed immediately to the hospital; they said that had we been a few minutes later, Little Jose would have died.

Little Jose never sent us a thank-you letter, and neither did he reduce his criminal activity. From that moment on, every time he committed a burglary and Spud was around, the other officers would remind Spud of that night. There were even gibes about

Spud needing to be charged as a party to the offence. After all, he had saved the burglar, enabling and abetting him to continue committing further burglaries.

On another occasion I found Little Jose in the back of a truck with a group of mates, drinking champagne from a case of a dozen bottles. I was immediately suspicious, as the previous day a dozen bottles of champagne had been stolen in the area, along with a lot of other property.

Little Jose claimed that he and his mates had returned from up north and had bought the champagne from a pub on the way back. They knew I was aware of their whenua in Te Hāpua, near the top of the North Island, so this had at least some small fabric of truth about it. Most accomplished liars like to include as much truth in their false stories as they can, and Little Jose was certainly an experienced liar. He was also a cocky chap who figured that his story would be hard for me to rebut. Bristling with confidence, he accompanied me — and the champagne — back to the police station.

Back then, the situation between criminal and policeman played out like a theatrical exercise with a script that was known well to both parties. Little Jose and I had performed it many times before. He knew the champagne was stolen and he knew that I knew he had stolen it.

The first act was for Little Jose to find out how much I actually knew. Did I know where the champagne was from? The criminal's code was that you did not confess to something unless the police had you cold. If the police did have the goods, it was acceptable to put your hands up and not lose face with your mates. To cough otherwise was simply not cool. That would result in a loss of street cred with criminal mates.

The second act was for me to convince Little Jose that not only did I know the champagne was stolen, but I also knew where it was stolen from. The burglary complainant lived in Manurewa and bought his liquor, including the champagne, from a local liquor merchant, Murphy's Wines and Spirits. By chance, the police club next door to the station also bought their booze from Murphy's Wines and Spirits.

In the third act, Little Jose would stick to his story to check whether I had any evidence and could prove that the champagne had come from Murphy's and, therefore, the burglary.

I left the interview room for a brief time before returning with the carton in which the champagne bottles were located. I showed Little Jose the unique Murphy's Wines and Spirits markings, which of course was proof that it had not come from up north as he had claimed. To further prove the point, I showed him the same label on boxes from the police bar. Being told that the owner of the burgled house had purchased his wine from Murphy's was sufficient for Little Jose to give a wry smile and tell me about the burglary — but not about where the rest of the property went, or who his co-offenders were.

Little Jose and I shared a little banter on the way down to the wooden cells and while I fingerprinted him once again. Did police bars help police solve crimes? Well, in this case, yes, they did.

Murphy's Wines and Spirits was burgled many times over the years and I suspect that the Jose twins were responsible for most of these, but we couldn't prove it. I did catch Big Jose in the act of burgling Murphy's one night many years later, after I had joined CIB. I was working night-shift crime car duties and on patrol early in the morning. Nothing much was happening, and at these times we often had turns at walking around the shops, called foot patrols, partly to try to catch some villain and partly to keep from falling asleep. This was particularly necessary for the observer, as at least the driver had something to do.

On this night shift I was the observer and needed a walk to clear my head; it was around 2 a.m. My offsider, Gary 'Catfish' Dunning, who I often partnered with on crime car, parked a little distance away from Southmall in Manurewa. I wandered through the shopping centre to the rear car park, which provided a view of the back entrance to Murphy's. There, I watched Big Jose for some time as he put a jack under Murphy's roller door and started cranking it up far enough for him to slide underneath. A pair of bolt cutters lay on the ground nearby, alongside a large padlock that had been just as successful at preventing this burglary as the previous 20-odd padlocks.

This happened in the early '80s when I was around 30. Looking around, I identified a car on the other side of the car park that I assumed was occupied by Little Jose, and probably others. I was without a radio or cell phone, which was the norm for the era; there wasn't going to be any backup. Finally, I could wait no longer: Big Jose was almost under the door. I shone my torch on him and told him to assume the position. Big Jose bounced up off the ground, and threw himself against the wall with arms and legs apart in the manner seen in all the TV police dramas. He was no milksop, so clearly he was acting from sheer fright at the voice out of the darkness. He had also been watching the same police crime stories on TV as the rest of us.

This was too good to be true, I thought. And sure enough, it was — the lights on the car I'd noticed came on and it crept towards us. Big Jose grew in confidence as the car got closer and closer. I figured our presumed friendly working relationship was about to be tested at this early-morning meeting, and was beginning to wish it was Little Jose coming towards me carrying a pair of hefty bolt cutters, rather than his bigger brother.

The tables had turned: I was outnumbered three to one. As we began to discuss the stand-off, however, a uniformed police car swept into the car park from the north. It was the night-shift sergeant. The result was that Big Jose accompanied us to the police station with his jack and his bolt cutters while his brother and other mate melted away into the darkness.

I still wonder how that meeting would have ended if backup hadn't arrived. A fight would have been one-sided — and letting me go would only have meant putting off the inevitable arrest for all three. The worst part was that I had allowed them to get the upper hand, to take control, even if it was only for a brief moment.

Decades later, after retiring as a sworn police officer, I happened to be lying in a ward at Middlemore Hospital next to a young Māori guy who was anxious to leave. I began talking to him, to calm him down as much as anything. He told me he was from Te Hāpua — so of course I asked him if he knew the Jose twins. He immediately knew who I was talking about, calling them the 'Terrible Twins'. He told me they had both passed away and were buried back up north, so would now be remaining at home and leaving the good folk of Manurewa in peace. The two were still together, even in death.

I have had time to review my dealings with them as I write. Their crimes were not 'petty' for the many victims of their criminal activity over many years. They were thieves and recalcitrant, recidivist offenders; typical criminals of the time. On the credit side, in my dealings with them they never lost their humour and always stopped to talk — unless of course they had reason to be running away.

While I got to know them well, as our paths crossed many times, I never tried to help them move in a different direction. I either locked them up or chin-wagged with them about nothing. What chance would I have had, though? At least one judge at Papakura, who probably saw the same personable potential in these young rogues, did try to help them change their ways, but they chose to ignore his wise words. Likely this reflected a life-long routine of ignoring advice from anyone in authority, including me.

As for the people of Manurewa being freed from burglary as a result of their passing, I knew this would never happen. Such vacuums are quickly filled.

LATER IN MY career, I did try to help a young ratbag from a criminal family in Papatoetoe. The father was bemoaning everything that life had brought to the family. He reckoned I should be trying to help them rather than locking them up. This struck a chord, so I thought I would give it a shot. I contacted a police officer who I knew had been a head prefect at St Stephen's Māori School in Bombay, South Auckland, which at that time was a well-respected college producing some well-rounded young men (it was later forced to close through lack of funding but more recently has been reopened; I wish it every success). We got this young guy accepted into the college, but after a few months of stolen cars being left around the school and other issues relating to dishonesty, he was expelled. I next encountered him a few years later, when he was a senior gang member on his way to prison — where he has since spent most of his adult life for serious criminal activity. This experience was not one I was in a hurry to repeat.

In any town or small city there will always be some families who commit a big percentage of the crime, and often they are large families. This disproportional situation is internationally recognised, not just a New Zealand anomaly. Dysfunctional families are a breeding ground for crime all over the world. Both the research and my own experience show that this may arise from a number of factors, including neglect, abuse, alcohol and drug use, mental disorder and poverty. If a male head of the family is abusive, violent, immoral and a criminal, with no balance from the matriarch, then the family will follow the only example provided. The next generation will turn out the same, and now you have a clan of criminals: brothers, sisters, cousins, nephews, grandchildren all following the lead provided by the older generations.

Poverty is a common excuse for all manner of offending, from shoplifting to murder. It is, undeniably, a factor, a genuine one in many cases. However, the generational criminal families often have a greater cashflow than their employed neighbours who are living a lawful lifestyle, scraping an existence together on meagre wages. Despite this, when entering the homes of many of these criminal families I often found very little furniture. Children would be sitting on the floor eating fish and chips off the paper they had been wrapped in. The whole place would convey the impression of poverty and, indeed, that was what the children experienced. With neither parent working this could be expected — but when the patriarch was detained regarding unpaid fines of over $1000, he would simply take a wad of cash from his back pocket and flick off the required amount.

Drug dealing and other criminal activity is a life choice — and only the children experience poverty. And when they are old enough, they follow the only example set for them.

4. DAN THE BURGLAR — THE REDEMPTION OF A PROFESSIONAL CRIMINAL

The difference between a long-term winner and a short-term loser is the ability to keep one's composure when the teeth of tension are lunching on your arse. — Dan Dudson

DAN DUDSON WAS A CLASSIC example of a recidivist criminal, a product of his background. He was known to almost every detective who had worked the top of the North Island since the 1960s, and turned up regularly during my CIB years. He was one of those colourful, larger-than-life characters who brightens up the dark moments of police life. I was not the only detective to fall for Dan's infectious humour and ready wit. The list of those with whom he got along included magistrates, judges, journalists, businessmen, lawyers — and just about any criminal of note. What was it that made him different to the dark array of relentless, nasty villains we police officers often saw? What set him aside even from the crooks with whom we *could* work and share a laugh?

Although it might seem a strange thing to say, Dan and I became friends — despite being on opposite sides of the law. But although notorious for the burglaries he committed, he had ethics. Dan placed great value on his word. It made no difference whether he gave it to another felon or to a detective. This was why he was held in high regard by the criminal fraternity who surrounded Dan for much of his life. They knew he would never grass on them, just as his detective friends knew that his word to them would stand the test of time. If Dan placed his trust in you, then you gained a glimpse into the principled integrity that lay behind his cheeky, outrageous and adventurous spirit.

In 2019, both Dan and I were writing memoirs. Mine became this one, while his would never be finished. At one point the plan was that Dan and I would write alternating chapters in a book we would produce together, although the whole thing eventually became too unwieldy. When Dan died, in 2020, his family found a large bronze chook and a card for me that he'd been intending to bring to a meeting with me the following day, along with a chapter for the book. Later I found an old computer disk of some of his earlier chapters. Dan was a talented writer with an eye for detail and a colourful turn of phrase. More than simply an entertaining account of an alternative life, his writing provides an insight from the other side of the cell door, and is a story I want to tell. The quotes in this chapter are from Dan's own writings, and I have drawn on his own descriptions of his life both growing up and as an adult.

It must be said, however, that there are hundreds of Dan's victims who would likely not appreciate a glowing testimony of a burglar who, over decades, broke into their homes and commercial premises with abandon and stole their precious possessions. I fully acknowledge that this charming man wronged those he stole from. There were clearly consequences to his theft that were experienced by his victims, and I do not wish to make light of the pain they felt.

DAN'S CRIMINAL HISTORY would easily be a book in itself. Sadly, it followed a well-trodden road — from Ōwairaka Boys' Home, to welfare foster homes, to Waikeria youth borstal, to the back of a police prison van entering through the large green gate at Mt Eden prison. He was there for the Mt Eden riots in the mid-1960s when he was not yet twenty, and his last visit to the same establishment was in the early 1990s. He spent time on prison farms like Rangipō, as well as Mt Crawford prison in Wellington. He also experienced a stint at Pāremoremo high-security prison.

Little is known for sure about Dan's family and parentage, but he was adopted by an elderly couple, the Dodsons, at birth (September 1945), and lived in Papatoetoe with them and their son Jack, his elder brother by some twenty years. Dan hated his brother, who treated him cruelly all his life and thwarted every step forward in the right direction. Dan loved his adopted father, Pop, but Pop and his wife were too old to control this spirited but lost boy who was seemingly tempted by the devil.

I also grew up in Papatoetoe, but on a very different track. While I was wandering around the schoolyard in a state of boredom, wondering what to do with myself, Dan, already out from school, was honing his art of burglary. He was looking for excitement and a life of adventure through thieving, not realising then that it would become like a drug that would not let him go. Once in the dark tunnel of crime, there were few if any exits.

Dan claimed to have started at Otahuhu College in 1958. Interestingly, David Lange, later to become a respected lawyer and also, of course, Prime Minister of New Zealand, was a prefect there around that time. While the rest of the school attended morning parade, Dan would creep into the prefects' common room and scoop up the cakes and biscuits from their lunches.

Military training in uniforms made of rough material that felt like sandpaper was compulsory every Wednesday. Dan and a mate began each Wednesday by dropping out of line on the military-style march around the streets; they would fall back in with the parade just before school broke up at three o'clock. After leaving the other marchers in the morning, they would run down to Māngere station and catch the train to Auckland, then ride the ferry to Devonport or Birkenhead.

So inspiring was the success of this wagging that it quickly led to Dan and his mate writing their own notes to the teachers, forging their parents' signatures. With the help of a little 'milk bottle money', which the pair collected from letter boxes during the night, they expanded their education to include the zoo and the movies. They also 'borrowed' pushbikes from railway stations for regular tours to unplanned destinations. And so Dan's criminal life began.

The headmaster at Otahuhu College was the well-known and respected Jock Leeming. He soon had Dan's number, and instructed him to remain after school to meet with a police detective. Dan recalled the long interviews with the detective, during which — in order to get home — he admitted to numerous crimes he hadn't committed, along with a lot that he had.

One day when he was told by Leeming to stay and wait for the detective was also the day that the pupils of Otahuhu College were scheduled to perform Gilbert & Sullivan's *The Pirates of Penzance*. All the tickets had been sold; the stage was set. The curtains were due to rise at 7.30 p.m.

Dan waited in the classroom until 4.30 p.m. Then he waited until 5 p.m., then 5.30 p.m. He began wandering around looking for someone to ask what was happening. Why hadn't the detective turned up? His footsteps echoed through empty college halls. Everyone had gone home. He wandered all over the school before returning to the main vestibule and knocking on the headmaster's door. No answer. Then he noticed a built-in window above the door, grabbed a chair and climbed up to peer through. Ten minutes later, he was over the road at the tuck shop buying two pies and some cakes. The shop assistant handed him the change — which he tossed into his pocket along with his other £600. The total ticket sales from *The Pirates of Penzance*. According to Dan, 'This was one pirate they would never forget again.'

The next morning, Dan was sent to the headmaster after assembly and was told he would be expelled. He ran off, stole a bicycle and was chased by the headmaster and prefects across the nearby Middlemore golf course as 'the spirit of Robin Hood and Dick Turpin took instant hold'. I don't think Dan had fully grasped the full concept of Robin Hood stealing from the rich to help the poor.

Clearly Dan was too wayward for his elderly adoptive parents, who were no brake to his already well-exercised criminal behaviour. Social welfare stepped in to put this boy on the road to redemption. Dan's new residence was Ōwairaka Boys' Home in Mt Albert. He was told he would really like it there, being with blokes his own age — around thirteen — and able to play table tennis and rugby, and that he shouldn't have been homed with the Dudsons in the first place.

The boys' home was full of roughnecks. Fights abounded. For the first month Dan went to another school by bus, but then for some unknown reason he wasn't allowed at school and never returned; it was the end of his formal education. During his time at the boys' home, two boys escaped from it. This resulted in *all* the occupants being punished for not advising the housemasters of the intended escape. Whatever blind faith Dan might have had in the boys' home was lost. He viewed it as barbaric. No one there had ever spoken to him about all the problems the judge said would be addressed. Any belief he had ever had in a system of justice collapsed.

Dan then went off to a number of foster homes, each providing him with completely opposite views on life, ranging from religious fanaticism to contempt of religion. He was dumped at each one by a probation officer. The only conversation related to how much payment the foster parent would receive.

'It was a bit like a cattle sale, but a definite advancement on the transportation days,' said Dan. 'I'd learned to identify Social Welfare and probation workers as nothing less than body snatchers.'

After being exposed to such contrasting influences, Dan was now totally confused. He felt he had been unwise to allow adults to toss him from one situation to another and it was time he took a stand. Spurred on by the negative feelings associated with being a bad adopted son, the saturated negative atmosphere of the boys' home, the embarrassment of ending his school days as 'dummy of the year' (his own description of how he felt about missing a lot of schooling and falling behind his contemporaries, despite being far from stupid) — his frustration with everything came rushing to the surface, forcing a personality change. Dan confronted the probation officer. The following week he was back home with the Dudsons.

Dan looked for, and found, employment in factories. He had begun setting himself up when his older brother Jack put a spanner in the works. He arranged for Dan to do another job elsewhere, which Dan hated. It caused friction at home because Jack, continuing to put Dan down as often as possible — would tell Pop how badly Dan was doing. As soon as the opportunity arose, Dan ended up back with his drug of choice. He hooked up with a couple of girls and a mate, and they broke into a shoe shop, where one of the girls left her fingerprints behind. Dan's mates split on him, resulting in his arrest, and he spent his first night in the old Auckland Central police station cells.

'I couldn't believe how much they stank,' he said. 'Drunks had been spewing all over the place, the toilets stank like only toilets can. The other cells reeked, and urine and vomit trickled out from under the cell doors on to the concrete walkway that was the exercise pen in the daytime.'

On 14 January 1963, aged seventeen, Dan was sentenced to borstal training at Waikeria youth prison, which is usually a two-year term — his record shows a couple of minor convictions in mid-1964 and early 1965, so he must have got out earlier. The same year he went into Waikeria, I was spending my last year on our family's farm. As far as I knew, I had yet to meet a criminal, burglar or domestic assailant.

DAN WAS A well-known member of criminal society for many years before I met him. It was at a coffee meeting that I found out from a retired detective, 'Mouse' Matthews, that Dan had been caught back in the 1960s by a Constable Harris after a burglary at the Dorchester Road dairy in the suburb of St Johns in East

Auckland. Dan remembered it well, along with the two trials (both for the burglary) where he was defended by Kevin Ryan (before he became a QC). At these trials was Dr Don Nelson, the government analyst who famously matched glass from the door of the dairy to fragments on Dan's clothing and proved something he called 'backward fragmentation'. Dan recalled that Dr Nelson stuck him to the crime even after his Pop had brought in glass from a window Dan had broken a week earlier. Somehow this only cemented Dr Nelson's case against him. Dan described the doctor as: 'A walking book of boring academic qualifications armed with a smorgasbord of pinpoint-accurate conviction stickers. I felt like a living dartboard every time he opened his mouth. The bastard was legal poison.'

Dan had a number of stories involving Constable Harris from East Auckland, who'd arrested him for the Dorchester Road burglary. He reckoned Ken Harris was the reason he stopped committing burglaries in the eastern suburbs of Auckland — it seemed that Constable Harris was always turning up when Dan was out sniffing out potential burglaries there.

Dan also recalled being on remand (for the Dorchester Road burglary) in Mt Eden prison when riot erupted in 1965. It has been suggested by other prisoners that Dan was responsible for getting the keys at the start of the riot, but he would never confirm or deny this. There were no charges against Dan arising from the riot. My research indicates that he would have had little, if anything, to do with it. He was still only nineteen years old and not in the clique of the older 'heavies' in Mt Eden at the time.

When Dan returned home from his prison sentence for the Dorchester Road burglary, he took on legitimate jobs, but the temptation to steal was never far away. While still young he could not see past the easy money obtained from burglary; and, of course, there was the excitement factor. After a short while, he was on the run.

One of Dan's main pursuers on this occasion was the man who became my mentor, Murray 'Muzza' Jeffries. Like me, Murray spent his early years on the Hauraki Plains before moving to South Auckland, where he attended Otahuhu College. He was older than Dan and they were not at the college at the same time. Murray was a fine athlete, representing New Zealand in the high jump at the Empire and Commonwealth Games in 1954 at the grand age of sixteen years. His high-school high-jump record remained intact for over twenty years. At sixteen he was already rated the third-best high-jumper in the world. Murray also coached athletics. One of his college trainees was a girl called Caryn Bird.

Along with Detective Len Johnson and Detective Sergeant Jim Toothill, Murray located Dan in 1969 after many adventures; he had been on the run for several months. Dan's partner during this time was, coincidentally, Caryn Bird, who was pregnant — in the end, Dan gave himself up for Caryn's sake. He had left his previous partner, Rusty, for the younger Caryn, and later left Caryn for a younger partner, Ruby; but remained on good terms with all three. Dan was soon back in prison again, this time with over 100 convictions for burglary, along with numerous thefts and unlawful taking of motor vehicles; a record at that time. While in custody, he also admitted to a further 200 or so such crimes. Dan and Murray remained friends for many years, but Murray eventually gave up on him when he continued to commit crimes.

In August 1974, the largest art burglary in New Zealand history (at that time) occurred at the apartment/museum of the industrialist George Wooller in Remuera, Auckland — just a few weeks after

Wooller had had a stroke which left him partially paralysed and unable to communicate clearly. A 'cat burglar' reached the third storey by moving from balcony to balcony before levering open a sliding door to gain entrance. Stolen items included antique Māori and Polynesian artefacts and a priceless gold honeycomb sculpture reportedly weighing a number of kilos. This last was Mr Wooller's prize possession; it had apparently taken years to create. The total value of the stolen property was assessed (initially, at least) at $400,000.

Detective Inspector R.B. 'Boof' McCarthy led a large team of detectives investigating the burglary, which culminated in a raid on a large city hotel in which most of the artefacts were recovered. One of those involved in this raid was Detective Sergeant Bryan McKenzie.

'Eventually an underworld informant came to light,' McKenzie recalled in an email to me, recounting the story for this book. 'We learnt that the goods were in Auckland and the criminals were looking for a buyer. We figured we would provide one. After a number of unsuccessful tricky and convoluted attempts to trap the offenders, and a false start to recover the artefacts using police in the guise of Australian criminal receivers, it was finally all organised.' The police set up a base, Big I, in the Intercontinental Hotel, which was just up the road from the High Court. An undercover officer received the desired call on a designated pay phone and gave the caller the name of the hotel, the room number and a contact name. Two officers, including McKenzie, were in the adjoining room and the hotel was surrounded by police. As the sting unfolded, the police burst in through the door of the undercover officer's hotel room. 'We were armed, and the man began to take a pistol from his pocket but thought better of it,' McKenzie told me. 'The man with the stolen property was, of course, the redoubtable Desmond Forrester Dudson.' He had with him a number of stolen artefacts — but not the golden honeycomb. 'We were later told it had been melted down by unknown persons in the underworld, who had then sold the gold. Wooller was distraught.'

At trial in October, Dan pleaded guilty to receiving stolen goods; he was sentenced to three years for receiving and six months for being 'armed with felonious intent'. The firearms sentence seems a bit light, given the circumstances, but perhaps it was a result of the guilty plea.

One question remains unanswered: who was the actual burglar? I suspect, myself, that Dan was the burglar — based on the fact that he was the burglar of note at the time and Ruby, his then partner, saw the golden honeycomb before it got melted down. If someone else had been the burglar and Dan just the receiver, it's doubtful that either he or Ruby would have sighted the honeycomb. The others involved would have dealt with it before passing the remainder of the goods on to the receiver for disposal.

I MET DAN in the early 1980s, when he helped persuade a young man to give evidence in a murder committed by his brother. After this I dropped in on Dan from time to time if I was on a quiet night shift. At the time he and Ruby were living in Papatoetoe. He was a night-time burglar and had become accustomed to sleeping most days and 'working' nights — or at least being awake in the early hours. I would use an agreed password on the police radio, which he was always listening to. Five minutes later he would have a coffee on. This also gave him a few minutes to hide any stolen gear that might have been lying about the house. If I had turned up without warning when he was storing stolen property, he wouldn't have let me inside without a search warrant and I would not have been welcomed back.

We had a number of early-morning chats during this time, but not with him as an informant. Being old-school, it would have gone against his ethos of standing by his word. His word, Dan said, was all he had left. It was important regardless of who he gave it to — associate criminal, or detective. Instead we spoke of people we both knew, prison life, criminal behaviours, and interesting stories. I learnt quite a bit from such discussions.

I lost track of Dan during the late 1980s, but around 1991 he found himself in the cells in Papakura where I was the detective sergeant. I brought Dan out of his cell and we sat down to talk about the previous few years and his recent experiences with the Waikato detectives.

Dan had been down near Matamata way, in Waikato province to the south of Auckland, and had been dodging a few well-known detectives in that patch. He had built himself a hut up in the Kaimai Ranges where he had been growing cannabis, and had hung a sign by this hut naming it 'Hoochie Min Trail'. He came out of the hills at night to carry out burglaries to keep his larder and liquor cabinet full. He also stole fuel for his stolen generator.

Dan admitted to those burglaries, as he had done with the hundreds of other burglaries he'd admitted to Murray Jeffries over twenty years earlier. He admitted all he could remember, or that we had some evidence for, but there were very few goods to return to the complainants. One of the houses he had burgled belonged to a fisherman friend of the detectives who were pursuing him. Dan would leave notes and cartoons, and send them letters with humorous quotes taunting his pursuers. The fisherman wanted his lucky fishing vest returned; I promised the detectives I would do what I could to assist.

Unfortunately for Dan, he had been caught not only with a large amount of cannabis and stolen property from burglaries, but also with a few firearms. He claimed they were for shooting deer and possum. However, the courts take a dim view of cannabis and firearms together. Given these circumstances, bail was unlikely. The reality was that Dan did have a fondness for firearms, but when they're coupled with a chosen path of criminality it makes for a bad combination: ethically, socially and when it comes to sentencing. For Dan the guns were part of his hunting lifestyle, but unfortunately for him he stole too many and was caught in possession of them too many times. He paid the obvious penalty when the judge's hammer came down at his court sentencing.

Dan and I had come to an understanding over the years. This was that neither of us would attempt to tell porkies to the other. When Dan told me a story about hidden jewellery in the Pureora Forest, I listened. He reckoned that a few years earlier he had committed a number of burglaries involving jewellery or had received jewellery, which he had buried in various spots around the forest. He planned to write a book in the form of a treasure hunt for people to locate the jewellery, but he'd got himself off track with his Hoochie Min Trail operation. The jewellery remained hidden in the forest.

If anyone but Dan had come up with this story, I would have thrown him back in the slammer and let him convince the judge of the veracity of the yarn. But he had not lied to me so far, and to my knowledge he never did. He may have stretched the facts, as any good storyteller does, but there was always truth in the message. He also possessed the type of adventurous Robin Hood nature that would come up with such an outrageous idea. I was also aware that

Dan often did bury his ill-gotten property; to this day, there will be people still digging up Dan's stolen booty all over the countryside.

I wrote a report to Dan's counsel to give to the judge, to get him out on bail and enable him to locate the stolen jewellery. What harm could it do? Besides, Dan had given me his word. In my view it was worth giving Dan a chance. I would be unlikely to write anyone else such a report. Most criminals' words and promises are about as useful as a dead fly floating in your tea.

Judge Richardson, known as 'the Bald Eagle', had a reputation as a person never to cross — as many prosecutors and defence counsel had found out to their cost over the years. Everything depended on his mood on the day. When Dan went to apply for bail, the Bald Eagle was clearly in a good mood and granted it, much to everyone's surprise.

Dan travelled south. On the way, at about 2 a.m. in the morning, he placed the fishing vest under the windscreen wipers of the fisherman's car before continuing south to the Pureora Forest with a metal detector. Much to his surprise, however, Hurricane Bola had been through the forest in 1988 and he could find none of his markers for the jewellery. I guess the fisherman was happy, though. Unfortunately for Dan, the judge was not so happy. After pleading guilty, Dan was sentenced in the High Court to a hefty three to four years' imprisonment. Dan's view of his sentence was typical: 'Justice has to be seen to be done and when you have been done by this justice system you have well and truly been done.'

The report I'd written was also an attempt on my part to get Dan a shorter prison sentence so he could help troubled youth with his talks. Dan had become genuinely keen to stop young offenders going to jail and wasting half their lives, as he had done. I had arranged for him to speak to some young problem kids at a local institution, where he was very well received. The leader of the group wrote a letter to the sentencing judge, but unfortunately it carried little weight.

Dan's view was that the young guys on the wrong road were more likely to listen to him than to people from authority, as the blinkers are immediately in place when those people speak. I had the opportunity to listen to a number of Dan's talks. He was a very compelling speaker, mixing humour with well-placed advice. There was no glorification of a criminal life.

On Dan's first Christmas back in Mt Eden I gave him two *Great Escapes* books. In return I received a pencil-dot drawing of 'The Fools Rush Inn', and a photo of Dan standing on the side of the road next to an official road sign about littering that said 'Thanks for doing the right thing' — taken during his trip to the Pureora Forest. It was his little joke about my report helping to get him out on bail.

Dan's partner Ruby became caught up in the periphery of his criminal activities. The cannabis was stored at her house, so she ended up in the women's prison next door to Dan for some time. They passed messages to each other via Morse code, by flashing their lights on and off, along with a loud call made nightly by Dan that was understood only by Ruby and some of his closer cellmates. The call was 'Magoorlie', the name of their family dog.

Time drifted on. While in prison, Dan somehow arranged for little notes to be left under the blotting page on my desk each night, no doubt hoping that I would believe he had escaped prison and made a midnight visit. I suspect he was getting them to my boss John Gott, who always beat me into work, although John never admitted it.

DAN WAS RELEASED from prison in 1994 and was never again charged with any crime.

He had always enjoyed the adventure and thrills of being a burglar. But later in life, after experiencing a few prison sentences, his natural intelligence reasoned that the fun part — the rush of adrenaline, the thrill of living on the edge — was simply not worth it anymore — and probably it never had been. I think that some of the company that had come with his life of crime was also a drawback for Dan. He described his last visit to Mt Eden as like being in a terrorist training camp compared with his earlier visits. Besides the brutal thuggery and the strong gang presence, for him the worst part of it was that he could not have an intelligent conversation with anyone. It was perhaps this, along with keeping his word to journalist Phil Taylor and myself that he would not commit any more crime, that drove him to change his ways. Perhaps the lasting memory of letting Murray Jeffries down also helped.

Around this time, Dan gave me his burglary bag, along with a note: 'Chook — inside here is the biggest hang-up you will ever see.' Inside the bum bag was a zipped leather pouch containing numerous different styles of lock pick, a perfume bottle, a packet of fireworks, a candle, pepper, a metal punch for shattering windows, tape commonly used for getting into vehicles, paper tissue for wiping fingerprints, etc. I am not sure if Dan gave it to me to remove temptation, or as an affirmation for himself and a declaration to me that this part of his life was finally over.

When Dan came out of prison, he needed to find a job — he was not keen on benefits because he was a conspiracy theorist. He didn't want Big Brother to know any more than they had to about his comings and goings. However, becoming legitimately employed would mean the IRD knowing more than Dan was keen for any government agency to know about him. He had difficulty trusting anyone in authority, which is a common-enough symptom in anyone who has spent long stretches of their life in jail.

There is no need to wonder where Dan's habit of suspicion and disbelief was formed. Reading his story of his childhood I saw that this time was clouded in confusion, spitting out a highly intelligent and inquisitive, but lost, boy. His naturally mischievous and adventuresome appetite was fed on the streets and at home with the wrong messages, including thieving. That led him to the Ōwairaka Boys' Home at a very early age, followed by the various foster homes, Waikeria youth prison, Mt Eden before he was twenty years old, and then on to Pāremoremo after the Mt Eden prison riots. All of these venues dragged him deeper and deeper into the worst of company. He learnt distrust, but sought stability and something meaningful and decent. Unfortunately, each time he got somewhere near it, he fell back into what was his learnt trade and the easiest way to make a living.

'The grey area preceding crime,' he wrote, 'is a mental "no man's land" that preys on boys, taking a psychological edge. It rewards them with illusions of immense benefits and profits for small investments of time and motion. Even when the crime is actually only a sin, the formula remains the same. Rewards in seconds, paid for in years. This is what I did not see then and therefore could not discover for myself for many years. It also needs to be said that crime is a love affair more than anything else. Crime fills many an unidentified psychological need. It is this compensatory factor that creates the basis for the love of crime.'

Dan found out later in life that Pop was in fact his grandfather — and the brother he hated was actually his father. But even this family tree is in doubt, because there is another version that says that Pop was his real father — that he had an affair with Jack's girlfriend and it was from this relationship that Dan was conceived. This would explain Jack's hatred of Dan, a constant daily reminder of this affair.

This was the tangled web of lies that resulted in Dan's childhood of confusion. And he escaped from that only to fall into the arms of the justice system and 'The Grey Lady with the big green gate' — Mt Eden prison. His experience growing up was in stark contrast to my own childhood on the farm where, while the lifestyle might have been mundane, there was no confusion; only warmth and protection.

CRIME HAD BECOME Dan's drug, an addiction. His life's lessons taught him that he was a second-class citizen, an ex-convict tossed about in a world he didn't fit into. He knew it was all his fault and never sought sympathy. He simply couldn't resist the temptation, the excitement and the addiction. Dan wrote that: 'Crime is a life of its own, giving new meaning to certain aspects of life that provide excitement, mental stimulation, activate the imagination, empower you with specialist knowledge and the faculty to accept the downside of crime, as if it were merely a hazard of the job. Crime is a state of mind, a mental sickness with a logic all of its own that overrides all other logic and is able to keep its host captive.'

The following story, told to me by Dan, best illustrates his fatal flaw of having no handbrake when that irresistible moment of temptation inevitably arrived. He had been serving time at Rangipo prison farm. The top job there was being a stockman, which, Dan said, was mainly reserved for older crims who were serving long sentences and to inmates who could be trusted. 'Being a stockman meant riding around on a horse keeping troughs clean and drains flowing, as well as helping with dehorning, de-knackering and shearing sheep.'

One day Dan, who had scored this top job, met a tourist — to whom he sold a prison horse in exchange for a bottle of whisky and a carton of cigarettes. This resulted in a charge of horse theft. Dan lost his privileged position and ended up in Mt Crawford prison. For the rest of his days Dan wondered why he had made such a poor decision.

He was certainly no angel. He knew this and did not hide from it. I always figured his saving grace was that, apart from a good dose of the smarts and his fantastic sense of humour, he kept his word regardless of who he gave it to. He had his own set of ethics to which he stuck firmly. Dan never broke into houses where there was someone home. For him, this was part of being a professional burglar and he took pride in it.

One matter that arose in my own talks with Dan was the matter of burglars intruding into private homes and lives. When I told him that going through women's underwear drawers looking for jewellery, which was commonly hidden there, was a gross breach of privacy, he couldn't understand this. When I also told him it resulted in many women burning the underwear as a result, he was stunned. From that day onwards I think he found it hard to comprehend that some bridges just cannot be crossed.

Shortly after his last release from prison, Dan approached me regarding a burglary of a jewellery shop in Newmarket, which involved antique and heirloom jewellery. Because of the personal nature of some of the jewellery, he wanted to act as an intermediary, at no profit to him, between the burglar and the police so that these items could be returned to the owner. While this sounded like a good idea to Dan, I knew it was never going to be acceptable to the police because of the precedent it would create. I approached the detective inspector in Newmarket. As I'd anticipated, he wouldn't have a bar of it. I didn't blame him. Dan then approached a large insurance company, NZI. Trevor Smith, then NZI's general manager, also refused to agree to the idea, for the same reasons, but he was so impressed by Dan's audacity and backstory that he employed him as a crime consultant. This put Dan on to the next phase of his rehabilitation journey: a speaking circuit as a security expert. A star was born; he was immensely popular as a speaker, though Dan doubted whether many of them put his advice to practical use. At one of these events, the annual conference of NZI managers, another of the guest speakers was All Blacks coach Sir Graham Henry. All attention was centred on Sir Graham until he turned to ask Dan what sport he was best at. In typical Dan style, the former burglar replied: 'Running — mostly away from policemen.' From that point on, Dan was the centre of attention.

As part of his crime consultant role, Dan would be tasked with defeating 'unbeatable' security systems. One time he bypassed a 'burglar-proof' alarm system by wearing a wetsuit; a new, 'unbeatable' acoustic house alarm developed in the US was also sent by Trevor Smith to Dan to test, and again he beat it. By this time Smith was working in the UK, and Dan was about the only person back in New Zealand that he kept in touch with.

IT IS INTERESTING to discuss the stress buttons for Dan compared with most people on the straight and narrow. When he was released for the final time, Dan found going straight difficult after a lifetime on the opposite side. Little chores such as arranging insurance, a warrant of fitness or a driver's licence — tasks that for others are routine — were stressful for him. Given all the efforts he was making to change his life completely, he was puzzled that the authorities wouldn't help him with petty infringements such as traffic tickets. Remember, this was the same man who was not stressed about moving stolen gear out the back door while the police were coming through the front.

But Dan's life had taught him many lessons, one of which is encapsulated in the quote I opened this chapter with: 'The difference between a long-term winner and a short-term loser is the ability to keep your composure when the teeth of tension are lunching on your arse.' This applies to people in all of life's circles. It's a quote I have stolen and used on many occasions when dealing with winners and losers over the years.

It is difficult to understand how honour could be associated with this character who viewed most policies and ideas from authority, whether political, judicial or medical, with an outrageous and humorous suspicion and saw conspiracy in everything. Here was a person who had burgled too many houses to count, had been involved in notorious incidents such as the Wooller burglary and the 1965 Mt Eden riot, had been involved in famous court cases, and associated with some of New Zealand's worst criminals. Yet when Len Johnson — a detective he knew and respected — died, Dan broke into Detective Sergeant Murray Jeffries' car which was parked outside his home. He left a condolence card for Len's wife and a note to Murray: 'Sorry about Len, I did not want to disturb you, as I could see you had visitors.' Afterwards he locked the car again. He knew that Murray was a close friend of Len's and would pass the message on to his family.

Ruby had a simple explanation for Dan's life of thieving: he was living the life he loved and on his terms. In Dan's own words, he had always been a nocturnal animal. He became hooked on heroes such as Robin Hood and Dick Turpin, so began living the part. 'I grew up too quickly. Thieving was such an exciting contrast to the boredom of school life. The desire to become a criminal captured my spirit,' he said.

Perhaps, though, he finally actually grew up. There was a meeting with the owner of a house he had burgled, which finally made clear to him their sense of personal intrusion following the burglary. Prior to this it seemed that Dan hadn't paused to think about the personal impact his theft would have on his victims. As far as he was concerned back then, it was only theft and the big insurance companies would come up with the dosh to reimburse the victims. In his senior years, however, he looked back at what he had done to strangers — and what he hadn't done for those dependent on him: Rusty, Caryn and Ruby, along with the children he had fathered to each of them. Going straight, he finally achieved something worthwhile for himself — self-esteem.

But whichever explanation is true, I'm certain that his humour and resilience got him through the dark times that punctuated his life. Dan may have been a bad man for much of his time on Earth, but he did redeem himself by spending his last 28 years without having to answer the question 'Guilty or not guilty?' It was satisfying to see that such a turnaround was possible. Dan found redemption, respect and self-worth by touring the country for many years, using his specialist skills of crime prevention, storytelling and his excellent communication. He garnered considerable publicity as well as making friends up and down the country and overseas. He had few obvious enemies, partly because he had a well-tuned skill of character assessment — a necessary skill for survival in prison.

If he didn't like what he saw, he dismissed the person with ease and moved away.

I MET UP with Dan at the Papakura police bar following the formal part of my first retirement as a sworn member of the police, in 2007. Some had not been keen to have him at the official function in case anyone present took exception. At the 'after match' function at Papakura station he presented me with a box containing a key, which had a metal tag on its key ring that read 'Return to the Onehunga Police'. It was the key to the old Onehunga police station. My first thought was that it clearly came from a long time ago when we were all so innocent. Dan told me that in the early 1960s, he'd stolen a motorbike from Papatoetoe in the early hours of one morning and took it for a joyride over to Māngere Bridge. Much to his alarm, he was stopped by an Asian policeman in Onehunga and questioned about the bike. Dan managed to convince the officer that he had a genuine right to the motorcycle, and was allowed to leave without spending the night in the cells. But before leaving he grabbed a set of keys the officer had put down when questioning him. It was over 40 years later that Dan 'handed them in' to me, and unfortunately the old police station in Onehunga had been replaced by a new station some years earlier.

This is typical of Dan — that even at the point of nearly being arrested, he was able to act spontaneously, mischievously and with a sense of adventure; and, some might say, unorthodox and outlandish humour. I immediately knew the identity of the policeman, because back in the 1960s there was only one Asian policeman in Auckland; he'd been a senior sergeant at Ōtāhuhu back in the late '70s and early '80s, so I knew him personally.

I tracked Charlie down, and he was presented with the key at a coffee morning for retired police, shortly after my own retirement. A cadet mate of mine, Lloyd Harris, organised the coffee mornings, so it was easy to arrange, but I doubt that Charlie was impressed with the story that went with the gift.

I had tried to get a cadet mate of Charlie's to present the key to him at one of their cadet reunions, but the mate refused — he didn't see any humour in Dan's behaviour. Fair enough, I guess; he was the detective who, with Bryan McKenzie, caught Dan at the Intercontinental Hotel in the early 1970s with stolen antiques and, more importantly, a firearm.

Dan died in June 2020, a day before he was due to have lunch with me to discuss his memories of the Mt Eden prison riot and the Wooller burglary. He had been working at his long-term job of providing security at a housing development on Auckland's North Shore, where he lived in a converted bus on site. Written on the front of the bus was 'End of Problem' and the registration plate bore his initials, DD. During the cold winter months, he took shelter in the local Pak'nSave underground car park to keep warm. It was there, while he was writing this chapter, that he had a heart attack. He died soon afterwards in an ambulance en route to hospital.

I don't think anyone realised the number of friends he had acquired along the way from all walks of life. A hard man with a soft side, a storyteller, and a criminal with a sense of honour. During Covid, Dan's employer, a large firm, had to put off workers from all its divisions, including Dan. However, he remained on site and continued to work unpaid. As soon as the lockdown finished, Dan was back on the pay roll. The firm planned to place a bench seat on this large building site, honouring Dan for his work.

I felt sad and disappointed, but not surprised, when I heard the news of Dan's death. He was a pig-headed bugger who refused to listen to anyone's advice regarding his health — his prejudices included resisting being given advice by his doctor. He didn't like being told what do by *anyone* in authority, which included not only doctors but also most judges, lawyers, media and all politicians. If he trusted you, he would give to you; but he chose carefully who he could trust.

Dan never finished anything. He would be close and protective towards his partner, but after a while he would typically walk away. His ex-partners still liked him, despite Dan having acted irresponsibly towards them and towards his children. Whenever things became too hard, his tendency was to walk away. He was happier on his own, which is where he ended up.

A deeply flawed man, but also a likeable rogue.

5. JOINING THE CIB, AND THE FIGHT FOR SOUTH AUCKLAND IN THE 1980s

BY THE MID-SEVENTIES PAPAKURA HAD become a district in its own right, separate from Ōtāhuhu (which later changed its name to Manukau). Later again, in the 1990s, the two districts merged again to become Counties Manukau District.

In 1975, at the age of 23, I was considered a senior member of staff at Papakura station and served as an acting sergeant for a short time. This ended after an altercation arose during the overstayers' fiasco in the mid-1970s. This unpopular government initiative introduced by Labour in 1973 and again by National in 1975 was driven by increased unemployment during the recession of the early 1970s, which was blamed in part on the many overstayers in the country. Those targeted were Pasifika. The operation was later referred to as 'the dawn raids' (1974–76). All police staff at Papakura station were called into work to be briefed by the district commander on our duties — which arose from a political decision to have us work with Immigration Department officials to remove all illegal overstayers from the country.

After the meeting, Murray Jeffries (one of my mentors), advised us younger staff to steer well clear of these operations where possible, as they were a political diversion. In the 1970s there were few Pasifika people in Papakura and therefore most of the raids took place outside our district. As Murray had foreseen, this directive went sour soon afterwards. A police inquiry was instigated — junior staff involved in the raids were in the firing line.

On this one late shift in 1976 when I was acting sergeant, a group of elderly, plain-clothed men stormed into the police station with the leader of the group demanding to know who was in charge. I asked him who he thought he was; the prompt and very terse reply I got informed me that he was a superintendent and had a couple of other commissioned officers in tow. It was an auspicious moment for Papakura: three commissioned officers at once in the station after dark. The district commander was meant to have informed me that all staff were to be ready at the station at a prescribed time to be interviewed over any involvement in the overstayer affair. Unfortunately, he failed to pass this message on to me, or to anyone else.

I don't know why, but high-ranking officers always seem to think they're known to every police officer in the land. In reality, at Papakura station we saw very few officers of any rank and that suited us fine. Arrogant bullyboys like this one were the reason we held that view.

After being abused by the superintendent that night, and then by the district commander the following morning for being disrespectful to the superintendent, I figured that maybe the acting sergeant job was not for me. I advised the district commander that as I could not read his mind nor receive messages telepathically, I did not wish to continue as acting sergeant.

This message was not well received. I found myself demoted to the watchhouse, which soon bored me. I was responsible for looking after the front counter, the radio, the telephones, the cell block and the teleprinter (which was about to be replaced by the 'Wanganui Computer', the new centralised electronic database for police). I felt like a prisoner in that watchhouse and was keen to get back out on to the street. The watchhouse also involved risks that I could clearly see, in the form of the safety of any inmates in the cells. These cells and their inmates were situated up the far end of the station, and often I didn't have time to check them as regularly as I was supposed to. I knew that if anything went wrong and someone died, by suicide or otherwise, I would be in the direct line of fire.

I clearly needed a change. After considering my options and taking advice from others who had been similarly caged, I applied to join the Criminal Investigation Branch (CIB) in late 1977. There I could return to hunting and interacting with criminals. After an interview with a serious CIB boss in Auckland Central, I was accepted early the following year and awaited the next CIB induction course, in August. After graduating from there I would go straight into the CIB.

THE CIB INDUCTION course at Trentham in 1978 was intense, with both academic lessons and study along with practical exercises. A few of the starting group fell by the wayside. Attention to detail (ATD) was high on the agenda. The course was followed by eighteen months of equally intense in-service training, in my case at Ōtāhuhu, along with regular examinations and reports from my CIB bosses in the field.

At Ōtāhuhu CIB we newbies were placed in a squad run by a detective sergeant. There were several squads: car squad, break (burglary) squad, drug squad and a general squad, which, from memory, was mainly fraud. We rotated through these squads over the next couple of years leading up to our detective qualifying course. And during that time we were expected to arrest as many villains who fell within our squad's criteria as we could. At least, that was how I read it.

My big bosses in South Auckland, Ron Chadwick and Brian 'Spooky' Middleton, were both trusted by staff who would follow them into battle anytime and anywhere. Both men were ruthless about any dishonesty and intolerant of any laziness they encountered in staff — as some detective constables discovered. These bosses backed their staff — at least the ones they knew they could trust — in whatever we did, provided it was done fairly with the goal of catching villains and serving the victims. If these broad outlines were followed, what we did would generally be sanctioned.

When a major incident occurred, such as a homicide, rape or armed robbery, members from all the squads teamed up to deal with it. Involvement in any long-running serious crime did, of course, affect our arrest rate, which was a worry. Of course the arrest rate wasn't a score; rather it was a check to ensure that we were actively pursuing criminals and not slacking. We were, in a sense, also on probation while we were checked to see whether we actually had the skill set required for CIB.

It was quite a learning curve. We all spent many hours in interview rooms with criminals who ranged from burglars, car knockers (aka car converters), fraudsters, druggies, sex offenders, robbers, murderers, and many others. From this I gained knowledge and, as a result, increased strength and confidence. If you ask any hunter how best to locate and snare their prey, they will tell you that first you must understand the prey's traits, behaviours, defence mechanisms and strengths. This gives you a better chance in the hunt. The interview room was where I gained much of that knowledge.

In the interview room, the initial invasion of the suspect's personal space naturally and automatically inspires discomfort. It is there, looking for the tiny signals sent out by the suspect, that the experienced detective thrives. These emotional responses are inherent; even people who are born blind produce the same expressions in the same circumstances. Problems arise when you encounter a sociopath who has no emotions or, more commonly, those who have spent all their lives lying so that this is their natural response to any question put to them.

Rarely was an interview the hostile, fierce physical interrogation — fists thumping the interview table — that many solicitors and, I think, judges imagined it was. Often after an interview, either successful or unsuccessful, officer and suspect walked to the cell block together with at least some understanding of each other. As such, it was a two-way street, and particularly useful for any half-clever detective who wanted to better understand those he dealt with daily.

Unfortunately, the development of this personal understanding and great education for police, as well as the establishment of common ground with the criminal, has been lost. Today, interviews between police and offenders have become more of a clinical exercise that involves little humour or understanding from either party. Video interviews were introduced in the late 1980s, which also created a more formal environment. The introduction of the Bill of Rights in 1990 — with all the cautions that required — resulted in interviewees receiving repeated warnings that they did not have to say anything. So they didn't, and many still don't.

Perhaps the seriousness and extent of drug crimes has also been responsible for the loss of the entertaining humour that once existed in this environment where people from different backgrounds met, contested, and often found common ground. Importantly, it gave us all the chance to discover that generally we are not that different; that terrible foundations will send a criminal down a different road.

We also spent a lot of time with traumatised victims, families of victims, and witnesses, which was also an education. We would have dealt with some of the victims and witnesses in the category of offenders as recently as the previous week, while others had never had any contact with the police their whole lives. For various reasons, many people harboured a deep suspicion of police that arose from family, political, ethnic or work backgrounds. Others were intimidated simply by being in a police station. Clear communication was key to overcoming all of these challenges.

I attended many homicides, and many more near-homicides, that left men and women, old folk and children with wrecked lives. Many I have now forgotten with the passage of time, but others hold a place in my memory; perhaps because I learnt a lot from the experience, or they were too sad to forget, or a spark of humour has kept them in the forefront of my memory. I'm referring to black humour, which I think can be best understood by those who visit those dark, ugly places and need to recover from what they witness. I am sure the police are not alone in this. Those working in ambulances, at accident and emergency departments or elsewhere in hospitals, pathologists, the military, fire departments, and probably many others, will have relied on black humour just to survive some of the horrors they have witnessed.

PART OF THE CIB in-service training involved crime car duties. In 1979 this meant working two consecutive weeks solid on night shift, as the only CIB member on duty from Penrose in the north to Meremere in the south and from coast to coast. We were provided with a driver, who was nearly always the latest recruit out of training school with only a few weeks of service, so little or no knowledge of serious crime scenes. I was, for all intents and purposes, alone to deal with whatever serious crime came up. And I was still ostensibly a constable on trial in CIB. This, I guess, was the best trial of all.

The latter part of the week on crime car was always busy. Right on schedule, on Saturday night 11 November 1979, a rape was reported. I interviewed the victim, a very shy, innocent, polite Pasifika girl aged nineteen. She was well spoken, despite being, understandably, very emotional — she was particularly worried about her parents finding out about the rape. After being at the pub with work friends she had been taken to what she'd thought was a party, but which turned out to be anything but.

She was raped by a gangster who had only just been released from prison after a two-year custodial sentence for a different rape. At that time this seemed to be accepted as the usual sentence for rape, which speaks volumes about the judicial and public view of this outrageous and detestable crime in the '60s and '70s. I have always believed the sentence to be unjust; and, indeed, the sentencing period increased over the following decades. From the early 1980s, rapists received non-parole sentences. In the early '90s, preventive detention was introduced.

After obtaining a statement from the rape victim, sorting the exhibits and ensuring that she was medically examined, the hunt was on for the offender. The case concluded with him being pulled out of bed at a local gang house. He denied being involved. Being just out of prison seems to give many criminals a medical condition that prevents them from speaking much — if at all!

By this time, it was near to daylight and the early shift was about to turn up. On the promise of a good coffee, we managed to arrange for the local Black Power chapter, who had a house near the Ōtāhuhu station, to come down to us. They provided us with seven similar-looking men to stand in an identification parade with the suspect when there was sufficient daylight in the police car park. The Black Power guys were most upset when they saw the suspect; they knew him, even though he was from a different gang. We persuaded them to finish their coffee and continue with their commitment to the parade. This was testimony to the link that then existed between gangs and the police. I believe it was achieved after years spent in interview rooms in police stations around the country, getting to know each other.

The victim now had to identify the offender — face to face. There were no one-way windows as there are on today's TV crime shows. Over the course of the past eight hours, this nineteen-year-old girl had been raped by this criminal, then managed to find somewhere — in the dark, in an unfamiliar suburb — to contact the police; no cell phones then. She had undergone the interview process, told her parents, and been medically examined in a dressing gown in the local surgery by a male European doctor. Now she was standing outside in front of eight rough-looking gang members, with no screen between her and them, and pointing out the offender. This took extraordinary courage and resilience.

By lunchtime I had amassed a sizeable-enough file to satisfy the custody senior sergeant to hold the recidivist rapist in the cells until his Monday-morning court date. Then I was off home to catch some kip before the Sunday-night shift. I was hoping that this shift would be quiet, as I needed to get home early if possible, have a shower and then attend a defended hearing court case that had been already set for Monday morning. I believe I did manage to get home around 5 a.m. for a shower and return to court to ensure that my witnesses were present by 9.30 a.m.

When I arrived at court, the rapist asked to speak to me in the court cells and told me he wished to plead guilty. He subsequently did so. This meant that the victim didn't have to go through the ordeal of giving evidence at trial. Sometime later, when I returned her clothing to her parents, I discovered that she had fled the country and was not expected to ever return — at least, this was what I was told.

The criminal was sentenced to another two years' imprisonment for this rape; he was probably out much earlier. Years later, a repeat rapist could be given a ten-year sentence, plus preventive detention, and a minimum period before parole would be considered. Not so then. This was my first rape case, and I thought the sentence was appalling. I had assumed that the offender would be sentenced to at least seven to eight years of imprisonment. I was, at the same time, relieved that I was spared the embarrassment of informing that nineteen-year-old girl that after all she had suffered, and the fact that she would probably never feel safe again for as long as she lived, the sentencing of a repeat convicted rapist was dealt with in such a shameful manner.

Even as a lowly constable in CIB I knew that the police practical procedure was likewise primitive, and inadequate from the victim's viewpoint. Fortunately, by the time I retired as a sworn member of the police in 2007, things had improved dramatically since those dark days of 1979. The interview processes were better, as were identification procedures. Medical examinations of victims were undertaken by predominantly female doctors specialising in sexual crimes. There was support for victims leading up to and at the court case, and corroboration of the victim's testimony using propensity or similar fact evidence (which I cover fully later in the book). And, of course, there was more sensible and realistic sentencing at court.

Hopefully I played a role in these changes — I certainly spent many years trying. I do realise, however, that there is room for further improvement, both in police investigations and in the courts.

HAVING JOINED CIB, I was keen to progress to become a detective sergeant. Following good reports and successful in-service training exams, I attended a detective qualifying course in 1980.

Completing the course meant the end of in-service training and the commencement of my new designation of detective. The course had not been as intense as the CIB induction course. It provided a more practical agenda — working through historical homicides noting points of interest, as well as a test to find out if we were up to the highly regarded detective designation. This was the last course that took place at Trentham; the next one was held at the new Police College in Porirua.

Although Ōtāhuhu station had provided a productive learning

environment for my in-service training, I was happy to be returning to Papakura to work with Detective Sergeant John 'The Captain' Manning, Ray 'Spud' Smith, Gary 'Catfish' Dunning and Graham 'Skeeta' Skeet, among others. I was living in Manurewa, within the Papakura district, at this time. While some felt they needed to live outside the area they policed in, I held the opposite view. Living locally helped me to understand the community I was working in, and gain a balanced view of its people — good and bad — and how they lived.

The relentless and ongoing nature of dealing with bad people, being fed a diet of tragic criminal events and working with the perpetrators of these events, as we do in the police, can result in a warped outlook. Where I lived in Manurewa I had a Māori family as neighbours on one side, and Pasifika and European working-class neighbours on the other boundaries. We got to know each other and enjoyed each other's company. I was lucky that my neighbours were all good people. If a gang member had moved in next door, things might have been different. Some not-so-good families lived not far away, but by living locally I was able to see first-hand how people can struggle both financially and with bringing up kids amidst the pressures that exist in suburbs where many villains also live. I have sometimes thought that if I had instead been dispatched to Dunedin after training and had dealt with drugs, 'white trash' and university students, my view of life and criminality would have been very different.

Papakura station was just as busy as Ōtāhuhu. We attended so many rapes, robberies, drive-by shootings and murders — in between a busy routine of thuggery, thievery and general criminal activity — that many of the smaller cases became a blur. Some, though, still stand out all these years later. One such case was the

Forsythe Saga in the early 1980s, which I touched on briefly above; this was when I had first met the prolific burglar Dan Dudson. Forsythe was the name of both the offender and the victim, and it did become a bit of a saga. As it turned out, a teenage boy shot his brother and dumped his body off a bridge in Karaka, South Auckland; a third brother, encouraged by Dan, eventually told us the truth.

A group of us in CIB, including a couple of detective sergeants, had interviewed both these brothers and two of their friends for hours after the victim first went missing in circumstances considered by other family members to be out of character. But we all concluded that the missing brother was laying low because there was an arrest warrant out for him. We believed that the four people we'd interviewed did not have enough bottle between the lot of them to murder anyone. But we were all wrong. It was another valuable lesson — *anyone* can kill, *anyone* can murder, even young teenagers. Motives can be nebulous and obtuse and at times appear meaningless and very insignificant — except in the mind of the killer at the time they commit the crime.

Early in this homicide inquiry I bumped into Detective Inspector Ron Chadwick, O/C (officer-in-charge) of CIB in South Auckland, walking down the back stairs of the Gordon Road CIB office in Ōtāhuhu. He asked if I still believed the four interviewees didn't have the bottle to do it; I told him I'd believe it when they found a body.

His response was succinct: 'Well, they're pulling the body out of the water right now.' The lesson in this instance being that young detectives are very much a work in progress.

The offending brother died in prison shortly after conviction.

Most of the motivations for murder can be found in the Bible and the writings of the ancient Greeks: jealousy, greed, envy, power and, of course, lust. But for many, the reasons for taking someone else's life were so vacuous and shallow that they seemed to me to cheapen life altogether. Often it would be about little more than petty things that most of us deal with regularly in our lives — like who puts out the rubbish — which can easily be resolved with discussion or, at worst, involve a verbal disagreement. But because of psychiatric issues, use or abuse of drugs and alcohol, or just plain, unrestrained anger, common, everyday tasks can somehow escalate out of all proportion and lead to someone dying. Some offenders seem to have no anger impulse control or any sense of consequences; there is no red stop button in their make-up. I wonder whether there was ever such a button, or, if there was, when they lost it. How do people, young or old, reach the point where they are able to violently end someone else's life?

WE ALSO SAW cases of extreme and horrific violence that did not end a person's life but instead changed it forever. One example was a case in Māngere in the early 1980s. The motivation this time was control and power, as it often is with rapists. Our Papakura crew was on weekend duty covering all of South Auckland when we got a call about an intruder rape in Māngere. The offender had tied the husband up and made him watch as he raped his wife and mocked the husband's sexual inadequacy during the process. Before leaving, he wrote a message in lipstick on the wall: 'You were a great root — I will be back'. This was a rape with brutal psychopathic overtones.

We waited for him, just in case — and true to his word, he returned to the victim's house and was arrested.

I interviewed the female victim— a remarkable woman, more concerned for her husband and how the rape had affected him than she was for her own welfare. This highlights the fact that in the crime of rape there are usually more victims than just the principal victim of the offence.

During a short conversation with this female victim, a rape crisis counsellor made the mistake of rubbishing men in general. The victim tore a strip off the counsellor, who quickly retired from the room. The lesson: take a little time to assess the situation before you assume too much. Victims are individuals, not clones; not every victim will react the same way. While some feelings and behaviours might be common to all, people react very differently to traumatic events such as rape.

I learnt to tread carefully until I had gained the confidence of the victim and assessed her (it was usually a her) individual needs. In this case I realised that the woman felt she was much stronger emotionally than her husband. She knew she would have to help him through this invasion into their lives; perhaps even more than he would be able to help her.

We were not always so lucky with catching offenders. One such case involved a callous and brutal attack on a very independent 90-year-old woman in her own home in Papakura. I remember it for two reasons. The first was because we never brought the offender to court, despite knowing who it was. You always remember the cases you lose. The second reason was the tragedy that followed.

The attack took place in the middle of the day; the victim was beaten unconscious and not found until the following day. She was hospitalised for some time and was unable to describe her attacker. We did, however, identify the offender. He was a psychologically disturbed and dangerous young man whom I had dealt with on a number of previous occasions for offences which never seemed to have a rational motive. This time, we located his fingerprint at the scene. But unfortunately, while the fingerprint identified the person, it was two points short of the minimum number of identifiable features required legally for court evidence and this twisted individual walked away from justice. We had to take it on the chin and move on, all the time knowing that the victim could not.

I heard from the old woman's family that she was devastated and could not live alone anymore. Her independence, of huge value to her, had been stolen and she died very shortly afterwards, in a retirement home, heartbroken. Meanwhile, the lowlife responsible for the invasion into her previously fulfilling lifestyle was walking free. He left Papakura, but I saw his name pop up in West Auckland a number of times after that.

Not all investigations are successful. Although I was gutted at the time, there was little I could do to change the outcome; I just had to move on to the next case.

Repeat victims, of which we saw a few, need to see that justice works for them, however. One young woman I have always remembered for her strength of character in the face of repeated and horrific acts against her was aged around seventeen when I first met her. As a child, she had been sexually violated by her uncles. When she was around fourteen, she was raped by gang members in Pukekohe. Her mother had psychological issues and was not able to help her daughter overcome these early challenges in her life, or prevent them from happening.

With apparently no one to turn to — and certainly not her uncles — this young girl had veered off on to a very rough road. Not surprisingly, her attitude towards most people, including authority figures, was very anti-social. She had given birth to a child who had been taken from her by the authorities because she had spent time around gangs, drugs and criminals.

Haunting her always were the actions that her family and adopted family — the gang — had inflicted on her. She bore a 'suicide bangle' on both wrists, the scars clearly visible. After spending only a brief amount of time with her, it was obvious to me that despite her rough language, full of obscenities, she was a smart girl. Her intelligence continued to shine through her bitterness. Given a different start in life, she could have been anything she wanted to be.

In an attempt to straighten out her life and get her child back, she had moved on from the dark place she was in and had a straight boyfriend. Her life was about to take a step back into darkness, however. While out with her boyfriend one night, their car ran out of petrol near Manurewa. Along came a supposedly friendly man to help, but who turned out to be not only a gang member but also a rapist. He separated the two by taking the boyfriend off to get petrol from a friend's place; another gang member. He then returned, took the victim to a nearby bush area and raped her.

At this point in her life, this young woman had many convictions, including attacking police with a knife. I was able to convince her that if she helped me, together we would bring the man responsible to court. She bought into the mission to shut down the offender; we would give it our best possible shot in court. The reason behind this was simple: I really wanted her to experience that the system, both police and the court, worked for everyone — and this included her.

The timeframe of the crime was important because a police dog handler had stopped the offender just prior to him finding the victim and her boyfriend in their broken-down car. The clock was ticking from that point on. I carried out a time check to ensure that the timeframe created enough opportunity for the rape to have been committed as the victim had reported it in her statement. It was possible, but it was tight; there were just a few minutes to spare.

In the court case, the two critical areas were this timeframe plus whether the victim and her boyfriend presented as credible witnesses. There was no point in trying to present the victim as a saint, as her language would give her away as coming from a rough background. I had briefed her at length about how the court case would go and what to expect under cross-examination. As I suspected she would, she dealt with the court hearing cleverly and came through unscathed.

Unfortunately, the defence suggested to the dog handler that when he spoke to the accused it might have taken 25 minutes — and the dog handler casually accepted this 25-minute estimate. This time of 25 minutes became a fact, when it would actually have only taken five to ten minutes at the very most. The jury acquitted the accused. I saw their notes from the jury room where they had worked through the timings, and that 25 minutes was the decider.

Once again, this victim had been disbelieved by society. I learnt that justice is not always served in court; it can founder on a small technicality or minor error in evidence. I was not angry with the jury's decision as much as I was with myself for not tightening up on this loose piece of evidence. This was the only rape trial I ever took to the High Court and lost. I berated myself for not having briefed the dog handler more effectively.

If only it had not been this particular repeat victim. I had expected her to be upset, but instead she thanked me for believing her and told me that we had done the best we could in the circumstances.

Many years later, she rang me about some other problem. Most people with her history would have had the positive aspects of their character destroyed, but she was still perky, and taking the setbacks and challenges in her stride. Despite the scars she bore, both physical and mental, she had moved on. A tough, smart woman and a survivor.

THERE WERE MANY other homicides and vicious assaults in the turbulent '80s in South Auckland. It was also at this time that a serial rapist was active — but swept up as we were by the day-to-day turmoil we were dealing with, we were unable to join the dots and spend time tracking him down. This offender continued to build a very substantial trail of victims through the 1980s and into the 1990s. He became known as the South Auckland or Park rapist, or 'the Ghost'. Our hunt for him was not only my biggest case to date but also aroused both national and international interest.

6. OPERATION PARK — THE HUNT FOR THE SOUTH AUCKLAND GHOST

STAFF MEMBERS IN THE PAPAKURA CIB office were in continual flux during the '80s as staff took promotions or were transferred to other branches, and other staff arrived to replace them. South Auckland was well known as a great training ground, in part due to the high crime levels, and many used it as that before moving on for their family's sake and to make a more visible difference in the provinces. It meant an enormous turnover in staff, and staffing issues were always present.

In 1985, John Manning left Papakura to take up a more senior role in Auckland Central, and I was promoted to detective sergeant in Manning's place. This was the rank I had aspired to from the moment I joined CIB, and I was content to remain in this rank for the remainder of my career. Apart from being another step up the ladder to avoid being the tea boy, it also provided me with more opportunities to take the lead in serious crime. And remaining there enabled me to avoid much of the office politics and administrative bureaucracy that held no interest for me.

Around 1987, John Gott, known to most of us as 'Gotti', arrived in Papakura, bringing with him national police experience. (Sadly, he died in 2017.) We formed a successful CIB team over the next half-dozen years, encouraged to find the truth from a crime scene — exhibits, forensics, interviews — while at the same time looking after the victim; and then begin the hunt for the offender. Hunting down criminals and putting them before a court could be trying and was, of course, not always successful. But solving the crime was a personal challenge for me, and given the knowledge of the victims and their trauma it was not difficult to be enthusiastic about this task. Not only was it our duty to the victim and the public, but there was also the personal satisfaction of a successful outcome.

Gotti arrived in time to be 2IC for the Red Fox Tavern homicide, in which the publican was shot dead in front of his staff by two robbers, at closing time. I was O/C Scene. The initial inquiry went on for months, though the offenders weren't convicted until more than 30 years later. This is a classic example of unfinished business: unsolved murder and rape files are never 'dead' even after the original investigating officers have retired. We owe closure to the families and those directly involved; efforts to investigate these cases are never abandoned.

The workload remained heavy into the early '90s. Many of the serious crimes were committed by career criminals and gang members, and they slipped from the memory quickly not because they were unimportant but because they became routine. Not so others — one morning around 1990, a man picked up a knife and randomly stabbed a primary school girl cycling to school in

Manurewa; she sustained critical injuries and her outlook was poor. This type of crime, obviously, provokes strong emotions and created much angst over the whole country. I was 2IC on this one, and as such gave direction to the inquiry. Sitting in my office at the end of the first day of investigations, preparing the programme for the following day, I heard over the police radio that someone in the general area where the attack had occurred was being pursued by a dog handler. Detectives learn early not to believe in coincidences; I headed to the scene, and sure enough it was the offender. Even though at interview he confessed to the crime, he could not explain why he had done it; just a little worm in a corner of his brain. He was declared insane; the young girl survived to live with her memories.

In effect, we were never off duty. I had just got my head on the pillow at 11 p.m. one Sunday night early in 1991 when I was called out to a homicide at the top of the Āwhitu Peninsula, about an hour away from home. When we arrived at the isolated beach property it was pitch-black and we viewed the deceased woman by torchlight. Clearly we could do nothing until daylight — except that my torch picked up a note reading 'the other body is in the barn'. It was so dark we couldn't even see a barn, but eventually we stumbled upon it to find a badly wounded man sitting on a hay bale. We helicoptered him out as the Armed Offenders Squad flew in to guard both the scene and us. Not much sleep was had that night. In the morning, the offender was located at a nearby beach and arrested. He was the estranged husband of the dead woman, who had flown in from Australia to kill her and her alleged boyfriend.

IN FEBRUARY 1993, one of the scenes we attended was an intruder rape complaint in Weymouth Road, Manurewa. The intruder had entered through an open window, tied up a 40-year-old woman with ripped-up strips of her favourite dress, taken from the clothesline, then sexually violated her. During the rape he held a knife, also taken from the house, to her throat. The offender then raped her twelve-year-old daughter in three different locations in the house while the mother was tied up and powerless to intervene. It was a particularly brutal and sadistic attack. We had only a very vague general description of the offender, who had brought with him some muslin material used in tandem with the strips of clothing to control his victims.

There had been no incidents in the area that could be considered as precursors. Living nearby was a known rapist, however, and he was immediately a 'person of interest'. His alibi was that he had been sitting alone in his car 80 kilometres away, on Auckland's North Shore, watching the rain fall from the heavens all night. We noted that he had sanitised his car the morning after the attack — this was significant because he had been caught for his previous rape through forensic evidence found in his vehicle. A search of this man's house turned up muslin similar to that described by the mother as being in the possession of her attacker.

We had no direct evidence, however, and the man denied any knowledge of the rapes. After taking a voluntary DNA sample from him, we released him — knowing that we'd be able to find him again when we needed him — and waited for a result that we hoped would confirm our suspicions. I was aware of the role of DNA in solving serious crimes; it had been used the previous year in New Plymouth in the murder of Nora Sole by Gary Ladbrook, to great effect. But in 1993 it was still relatively new to police investigations in New Zealand.

Then, forensic biologist Sue Vintiner from ESR came back to

us with a surprising and disappointing result: 'You're looking at the wrong man.' It was back to the drawing board. Thinking about it later, I wondered what our first suspect really was up to that wet night in February. He was almost certainly not watching the rain fall while parked up on a beach.

We did continue exploring possibilities through other inquiries, but found ourselves in a hole with very few leads to follow up. In the meantime, there were other pressing matters in Manurewa that took precedence. It wasn't like we only had this new rape to consider — murders and other serious crimes don't stop because you have a serial rapist at work. In the first six months of 1992 Papakura had thirteen gun-related homicides, and the crimes kept coming. The workload was, and I believe still is, extremely high for the number of staff we had.

On another stormy night some months later, there was another intruder rape, also in Manurewa. A 40-year-old woman was tied to her bed and raped. This offender had also used items found within or near the home of the victim. Unfortunately, she could provide little description of the offender.

The night-shift crime car that attended this attack was staffed by Detective Nigel McGlone, known to everyone as Guido. (Nearly all of us had nicknames; one detective sergeant I worked with for years said after my farewell in 2007 that it was the first time he'd heard my name was David.) Guido rang me at home straight away, as it was obvious to him that this was the work of the same offender as the rape a few months earlier. Again, however, our inquiries went nowhere — even though we canvassed a very large area and ran covert night patrols along with all the usual police rape investigation procedures: checking up on known sexual offenders and recent prison releases, offering rewards and talking to informants.

This was followed by two rapes of young girls in their homes in the neighbouring suburb of Wiri, which had fallen to Lambo — now Detective Lamb — my junior cadet and old I-Car mate from a decade earlier in Papakura. Although Wiri bordered Manurewa, it was in Manukau police district and therefore not my patch. Lambo and I discussed the four unsolved rapes. We were as confident as we could be that they had all been committed by a single offender.

Then, during the worst storm of the winter, the rapist struck again — in Manurewa, near the location of the first attack. On this occasion the victim had ventured outside to see who was prowling around the house. She was raped against a shed in heavy rain before being dragged to a neighbouring park, tied to a tree and violated again.

We were now sure that a vicious serial rapist had materialised in Manurewa, and this would soon be confirmed by DNA. This offender was clearly an experienced burglar and rapist, but we had no one recently released from prison who fitted either the behaviour or the description. Could he have been raping women and girls elsewhere?

I recalled some detectives working in Ōtara and Ōtāhuhu five or six years earlier talking of numerous rapes in that area. So I drove the 20 kilometres up the motorway to Ōtāhuhu and visited the records office where these files were now held. I took every file relating to a rape or intruder attack — both solved and unsolved — that I could locate. The sheer volume of unsolved cases stunned me; they went back to the mid-1980s. I took dozens and dozens of files home with me and spent a lot of time reading and absorbing these files instead of sleeping.

It was hard to believe that there were so many unsolved 'stranger intruder' rapes involving young girls in their homes. But having worked in the area myself during the early part of the '80s I knew what a battlefield it had been. I hadn't attended any of these rapes myself — after I'd been promoted in 1985 I was no longer required to do crime car duties, and most of the offences had taken place after this date.

Almost all of these rapes had been filed as single events and not linked to one offender. There had been some suspicion among those working the area at the time, but — just the same as on my patch — there were few leads and the pressure of the next major event pushed the rape cases into filing. Now, looking at them all together, it became clear to me that the modus operandi — the way the crimes were committed — for most of these unsolved cases was the same as that of our rapist in Manurewa. The victims were predominantly young, mostly under 15 years old; the homes were similar in appearance, often next to parks, schools or walkways, and all in similar, lower socioeconomic areas. The entry style was the same, with a knife commonly taken from the house and used to gain control, and the same language was used. The rapes, or attempted rapes, took place with the victim lying on her back with him on top, wearing something over his face. Descriptions of the build of the offender were similar and he was thought to be Māori or Pasifika. There were no fingerprints left at any of the scenes.

Looking back, this marked the beginning of my behavioural analysis of rape behaviour. I was completely sure that these crimes were linked, but I had to convince others. I located three rapes that still had potential forensic exhibits in storage, and had Sue V at ESR check them against the DNA from our Manurewa/Wiri series. All of the three unsolved cases matched.

It is fair to say that this put a spotlight on the offences and became a persuasive argument for committing resources to catch this man. Not only had he been active for years, but his offences were escalating both in number and in the violence involved. I was determined that the offender was going to be in the cells before any of these cases were filed again.

AT LEAST WE had a bit more information now — we knew where he came from back in the 1980s and in 1990. He was likely to have been living in Ōtara in the late '80s and now to be living in Manurewa. This had to be a clue to his identity. However, there remained the big question of how to isolate and find that one person among many thousands. Where and how could we find common factors that would identify our offender, a man who seemed to slip in and out of people's homes with the eerie ease of a ghost?

Getting enough staff on the job continued to be an issue. In Manurewa the rapes continued through 1993 and into 1994, while we struggled to keep a team together to investigate them. Each time another rape occurred we would gain extra staff from Manukau for a week or so, but then they'd be gone and we'd be back to one or two people trying to solve this massive problem. Lambo was a regular visitor from Manukau. He became so annoyed at what he perceived as a lack of commitment by the hierarchy that he accused them at a CIB weekly meeting of not being committed to catching this man who was raping girls in their beds throughout South Auckland. He was taken aside and told to consider his future in CIB. He had to pull his head in and wait for another opportunity — but on the up-side, he'd made the point in front of quite a few staff and brought attention to what was going on. Hopefully the seed he had sown would flourish later.

While not known for his subtlety, Lambo was a relentless

investigator — someone you'd always want on an inquiry like this. I had worked the streets with him in Papakura in the early '70s and was aware of his street prowess as well as his enthusiasm and determination. These qualities sometimes landed him in trouble with those whose professional lives were instead governed by career aspirations and who didn't seem to feel the same pressure to push full steam ahead. Given the difficulty in obtaining the sufficient resources to do justice to the investigation, it felt to me as if we were marking time, waiting for the rapist to make a mistake — which he had clearly not done over the preceding decade.

Lambo and I both knew that what we needed was a permanent, focused team set up to catch this ghost before he raped any more women and girls. Not only were we trying to solve the rapes already committed, but also, at the same time, trying to prevent any more from occurring. And we were coming second on both counts. With every new rape that occurred we knew we had failed the public, failed ourselves and, more importantly, failed the women and young girls in the homes where they had expected to be safe. There was no way to avoid the knowledge that we were not delivering for them.

I vividly remember one of the rapes, which occurred in November 1993 in Manurewa. The youngest of the rapist's victims to date, she was a very pretty and clever little ten-year-old Māori girl. And she provided us with what turned out to be the best description of the Ghost — not that we realised this at the time. She was snatched from her home while others slept nearby, and marched a kilometre up the railway lines in the pouring rain before being raped at a nearby railway station and then released. Her feet got cut on the stones as she wandered back along the railway lines to her home in the still-pouring rain.

This latest rape made a total of sixteen on my list, but they were much more than numbers to me. Through interviews and follow-ups I had got to know each victim personally — or at least I felt I did. I felt as if I had a personal as well as a professional stake in finding the rapist. This vicious depravity just had to be stopped.

Some of the girls who had been raped came from tough backgrounds and had been only just keeping their heads above the muck around them — only to have the boot of the rapist land on their heads, pushing them back under the mire. Knowing this drove us harder, and the hours we worked were becoming longer and longer. While Lambo and the other visiting officers returned to their other duties a short time after each rape, I carried the case files throughout. I was not going to allow them to be filed as the Ōtara ones had been in the 1980s.

From this latest attack on the ten-year-old girl, we finally had a couple of witnesses crossing a railway bridge nearby who had seen a man place a chair under a window of the victim's house before walking back to another male. They were seen to sniff from what looked like a glue bag. Surely not a local glue-sniffer with a mate? It made no sense, but we put a lot of effort into locating these two men. Despite that, we could not identify them. We were a long way from solving these appalling crimes.

ALTHOUGH MANY DIFFERENT avenues of inquiry were followed into the beginning of 1994, Gotti could not, of course, put all our staff in our small office at Papakura into this one series of crimes. As well as the hunt for the Ghost I was also having to cover other matters and was constantly being pulled away from the task at hand. I knew that if the momentum of the rapes paused, as they did from time to time, I would soon be dragged into investigating something else. In a report to the district commander at Ōtāhuhu I made the request for a permanent squad, hoping for more staff from the larger adjoining police district, and the Auckland region in general, to assist with finding the rapist.

And then it happened. Early in 1994, while I was relieving Gotti and running yet another homicide investigation (a man had murdered his stepson before burning his body in the family incinerator), I was finally placed permanently on Operation Park — the name I had given to the hunt for the South Auckland rapist because there was a park near three of the early rapes in Manurewa. Perhaps my report had at last struck a chord with the Manukau district commander and the regional commander; more likely, though, it was pressure from outside sources that brought about the change.

I took all my folders containing the many rape documents to an office in Manukau. The cases now numbered around 30 and went back to the early 1980s. Fortunately for us, though not for Ōtara, the offender had moved his offending back to the Ōtara and Māngere areas around the same time — it meant that Manukau CIB, with its greater resources, was now in the driver's seat.

I was to work again with Stewart Mills, an early supervisor of mine and now a detective senior sergeant. The two of us against the world, was how Stew put it. There were a few others, of course. Finally, we had a team — albeit small — to work permanently on this hunt for the rapist, which by now had attracted national interest. Politicians were having a field day. Even with the slightly bigger team we still had nowhere near enough staff, but — a year after the first attack in Manurewa — at least we had some staff working solely on Operation Park.

Following some political interference, which for once I was happy to see, the operation finally took shape. Lambo was back with us after a stint in hospital. Detective Sergeant Brett Simpson, known as 'Simpo', also joined us to focus on suspects. Very early in his CIB career, Brett had been the clerk of the Red Fox Tavern homicide inquiry. The publican, 43-year-old Chris Bush, had been shot dead during an aggravated robbery at the pub on Labour Weekend 1987. The masked offenders could not be identified at the time and the case went cold (it was reopened and led to two men being convicted 30 years later). Simpo had been involved in many more inquiries since then and was well regarded.

Bringing our team up to five was a new tool that was meant to help us: a 'criminal analyst'. This was a new concept, and the district commander thought this man would solve everything on his own. Unfortunately, our analyst had no CIB experience, and although he was more switched on about computers than us, in our opinion he added little else to the hunt. One of his early inspirational forecasts was that the next victim would be a female and the offender a male. We were not particularly impressed. While the concept of a criminal analyst might have been forward-thinking and worthy, without any direct police experience this particular one may not have been the wisest choice.

The media were by now regularly reporting special updates on this series of rapes. In the main they were helpful in complying with our requests. But not always. It might appear to many people — and it was certainly a focus in the media — that a person wandering out of their home at night and coming back, often wet through, on the very nights when the rapes had occurred should be easy to identify. The reality was that there were countless thousands of men who lived in a twilight zone in which their absence would not be noticed. Some lived alone or with other criminals who came and went at will without alerting anyone. Others stayed on and off with different people, so their absence on any particular night would go unnoticed. We lived in hope that someone just might ring the police TV programme *Crimewatch* and give us the identity of the Ghost, but despite many appeals, this never happened. It seemed to me that I was forever on *Crimewatch* trying to encourage the one phone call that might make a difference. So much so that one of my cadet mates said it was more like *Chookwatch* than *Crimewatch*.

By May 1994, a few months after the operation had got properly off the ground, our team of five was still no nearer to finding our man. It was exasperating. Following an attack on a young girl in her home in Papatoetoe where she was severely beaten, the scene covered in blood, it was clear that we had to invest even more resources into this hunt. The level of violence appeared to be increasing and this caught the attention not only of the media but also national and local politicians. As a result, the pressure was on the police hierarchy, who could not silence this uproar as they had stymied Lambo a year earlier. Given the public and political outrage, this latest attack proved to be the game-changer in the hunt for the Ghost.

Detective Inspector John Manning was directed by the district commander to take over the inquiry. A respected and nationally well-regarded leader, John was an intelligent investigator with the ability to quickly get his head around a problem. I had worked with him for years and knew what he would bring to the table. Somehow, John Manning managed to lever Detective Senior Sergeant Peter Mitford-Burgess out of his job as O/C CIB Ōtara to become Operation Park's 2IC. Peter was a meticulous and organised detective with an innovative mind and a recorder, in detail, of absolutely everything. John couldn't have chosen better. I had been at high school with Peter, although one year behind him, but had not been in the trenches with him as much as I had with some of the others. I knew his reputation, however, and soon learnt what a craftsman he was in terms of his attention to detail. I was to work with him for many years. We called him either 'Mit' or 'Mitford'.

Meanwhile, Stew Mills was dragged back to Māngere, his old patch, where there had been a number of tricky homicides that required his oversight and which had suffered without his guidance.

I was the team's file manager, collating and reviewing rape files. Having been there from the outset, I knew them better than anyone. I also knew many of the victims, who called me frequently for help sorting out all kinds of domestic matters, from family issues to moving house after the rapes, to protection and a police presence for getting children to school. We helped where we could, though it wasn't always possible. Lives that were often already chaotic and dysfunctional had become even muddier after their attacks. Parents and victims were reaching out for the help that was now available in the form of the Park team. Many of these families had not previously viewed the police as allies.

Home was where we managed to snatch a few hours' sleep, and not much else. The investigation consumed us 24/7.

IT WAS NOW eighteen months since the Ghost's first Manurewa rape, and the rapes had continued regardless of the efforts and plans we put in place and the increased staff numbers. The attacks had moved back to Ōtara, then to Māngere after the bloody assault in Papatoetoe that brought John Manning into the game with an enlarged team. More than 40 women and girls had now been attacked by this prolific and violent offender. And traditional police investigative procedures and practices were simply not working; the rapist was winning. Even though we were computerised, had a dedicated typist team, a clerk, several investigators and a very focused and skilful inner sanctum, we were lagging behind. Not to mention our supposed criminal analyst, who I think even the district commander was now realising was out of his depth, and who John Manning had to gag after the analyst made an unhelpful unauthorised press release. (When joining the police, we were warned about the 'three Ps' which were the downfall of most officers at this time: Piss — Property — Prostitutes. I had now formed my new three P's to watch out for: Politicians — Press — Pettifoggers.)

Frustration and angst were building not only within the team but also in the community. The havoc being wreaked on victims, their families and the community at large was increasing with every day and every rape.

We had numerous phases ongoing in the investigation. These included the 'John Bull boot phase'. Impressions of this boot type — size 9–11 — had been found at a number of recent rape scenes. They were expensive work boots mainly sold to industry and provided to factory workers. In the John Bull boot phases we contacted the suppliers of these boots, regardless of size. All the factories that had purchased them in the Auckland area were checked for employees provided with these boots. These employees were then blooded. Unfortunately, not all factories kept good records, but we checked everything we could.

Along with most of the Operation Park inner sanctum, I was attending all the scenes of the incoming rapes. By now I was speaking to Sue V at ESR about the rapes on virtually a daily basis; blooding teams were regularly interchanged to keep staff fresh. Meanwhile I kept looking for more complaints and analysing the files we had, as well as dealing with all the victims who needed support and progress reports. All victims were interviewed at length in an attempt to find any link between them. On top of this, there was a lot of administrative work: regular updates to headquarters and the Manukau and Auckland hierarchy; managing the staff movements and replacements coming from all four Auckland districts as well as from outside the city; and fiscal reports, staff appraisals and responses to parliamentary questions.

We also plotted the attacks on a map — one large one up on a wall, and also a computerised version. This highlighted how easy it was for the Ghost to move about South Auckland without being seen. A network of parks, schools and walkways allowed him to keep off the streets where he could be sighted. We placed covert officers, hidden in trees, along these routes at night and in all weathers. Many single men were stopped by these officers and blood samples taken, but all returned negative.

Driving around the area targeted by the Ghost, we noticed that many people lived like goldfish in a bowl, with few houses having curtains. This was making it easy for the offender to find his targets. We tried to get the message out through newspapers, *Crimewatch* and TV news, but it became clear that these outlets weren't reaching our intended audience. So we dropped leaflets in letter boxes, requesting the occupants to make some effort to cover their windows, even if this meant hanging blankets over them. These leaflets were in every language we thought applicable, including Samoan, Tongan, Tokelauan, Niuean and Māori. Unfortunately, this initiative had little to no effect.

We were to learn the hard way that posting rewards brought out even more crazy ideas from the public than we already had and were very unlikely to bring the Ghost to the surface. I know now that offering a reward for information on a lone stranger serial sexual offender is unlikely to ever bring a result. These people act alone and do not tell anyone what they've done. Who would want to brag about breaking into a house and raping a young girl in her bed at knifepoint? These types of offender are usually loners (though not necessarily single men) and keep their secret, confused and twisted world hidden in their heads.

While at the time we were endlessly frustrated by our inability to catch this offender, what we didn't realise was that our efforts to find him would change the way policing of this type of crime in New Zealand would be done — forever.

7. DEVELOPING PROFILING DURING OPERATION PARK

OPERATION PARK IS CREDITED WITH showcasing the first use of criminal profiling to identify an offender in New Zealand, but that's not quite accurate. In 1988, Janine Law was found dead on her bed in Crummer Road, Grey Lynn, with a tea towel jammed into her mouth. Following the initial investigation, the coroner's verdict was that Ms Law had died after an asthma attack. However, many of the detectives and officers first on the scene were not satisfied with this verdict and they were supported by Ms Law's family.

After a number of attempts to have the verdict reconsidered because of anomalies, the file was finally sent to Counties Manukau police in 1994 to be reviewed. This was done by Detective Inspector John Manning (prior to him joining Operation Park) and Detective Senior Sergeant Steve Upton — a completely fresh pair of eyes, having not previously been involved in the original inquiry. It is not my intention to go into detail about this homicide and the differing views held by the original investigators and the review team, but suffice it to say the case was reopened and reinvestigated.

The view of Manning and Upton was that Janine Law had been raped and murdered in her bedroom by an intruder. They had the DNA of the offender from bodily fluids found at the scene, but where to start looking after six years when the trail was ice-cold? John Manning and Steve Upton suggested that investigators return to old arrest charge sheets and look for burglars and peepers arrested in the Grey Lynn area around the time of the murder. The team, led by Detective Inspector Steve Rutherford and Detective Senior Sergeant Jim Gallagher, carried this out and located one James Tamata, serving time in Pāremoremo prison for assaulting a woman he had attempted to rape. Tamata also had convictions for peeping and obscene phone calls, as well as two attempted rapes, since the murder of Janine Law. The charge sheet profile identified him as a suspect because one of his addresses was across the road from Janine Law's house. After DNA testing confirmed that Tamata was the offender, he confessed. He was later sentenced to life imprisonment.

Back at Operation Park, frustrated by the lack of progress despite many long hours of police work, John Manning decided to look deeper into alternative ways to locate the Ghost. His research took him to a new book written by British psychologist David Canter, called *Criminal Shadows*, which described different ways of locating a serial offender through what he called geographic profiling. John already knew something about profiling from the Janine Law case, but this time it would be on a larger scale with a more professional and detailed plan. In October 1994, he went to a criminal profiling seminar in Australia that proved very timely for us. There, John learnt from the FBI behavioural science group about preparing a profile of a serial rape offender based on his verbal, physical and sexual behaviour.

John now checked the files of sixteen stranger intruder rapists convicted in New Zealand, and found that certain characteristics matched exactly the findings reported overseas: all had burglary convictions before their first rape; they were all fifteen or sixteen years old at the time of their first crime; the average age at the time of their first rape was 25 years; and this first rape was in the area where they lived. As O/C, he decided that marrying the two profiling concepts — geographic and behavioural — together would now be the central focus of the Operation Park team. It had become clear that we would not get the answer from the public, or from the traditional investigative methodology we were using.

In November 1994, John gathered the members of the inner sanctum together, and in his quiet, methodical manner put the action plan to us. We listened with great interest; what might normally have been a hard sell was straightforward. It was clear that John had done his research and we all bought into the new direction for the operation. We were desperate for this after having scrambled for clues for over eighteen months and yet being nowhere near identifying the Ghost. Prowlers and night-time wanderers know their domain just as policemen on night shift know their beat: how many people in particular houses, which cars belong where, a strange vehicle in the street, etc. The Ghost was an experienced prowler. He was in control of his environment and felt comfortable within it. All we knew was that the Ghost was male, Māori or Pasifika, of slim to medium build and around the mid-thirties in age.

We had also recently learnt that our offender was still active — but the latest attack had occurred outside both Manukau and Papakura police districts, in Mt Albert. South Auckland was no longer his only area of activity. This was significant, because it opened up an even larger front and an area where suspects had not previously been investigated.

MOST EXPERIENCED DETECTIVES, including those on our team, were of course able to grasp the concept of linking crimes together by the unusual nature of the event and the modus operandi of the offender. But at the time there was nothing specialised regarding rape and, of course, the process also varied in accuracy from office to office and from detective to detective. At the time, serial rapists weren't something we all knew a lot about and certainly not on the scale of this one. We read up on the plentiful international literature and learnt on the hoof. We read *Criminal Shadows* and, when it hit the bookshelves in 1995, *Mindhunter* by John Douglas (a former FBI agent) and Mark Olshaker, describing criminal-personality profiling. Joseph Wambaugh's *The Blooding*, which told the story of Colin Pitchfork, the first person to be convicted of rape and murder on the basis of DNA testing, was also absorbed. I purchased all these books myself and still have those copies, along with many more published since.

Having read a fair bit, I was becoming fairly adept at linking crimes through behavioural characteristics, but we still had to put together a plan for identifying an offender through criminal profiling based on offender behaviour — *and* convince those with the staff and financial clout to get it moving.

Studying the verbal, sexual and physical behaviour of the offender gives you insights into the type of rapist, and clues to his identity. The FBI had various classifications of rapists based on behaviour. Our offender fell into the category of a 'power reassurance rapist'. This type of rapist is driven by sexual fantasy and seeks to dominate by surprise. He will often tell his victims he will not hurt them, but could become more aggressive as his series continued. He was also a 'marauder rapist', as defined by David Canter in *Criminal Shadows* — a rapist who marauds out from a base which is usually his home, workplace or 'bolt hole'. Canter explained how studying the geographic spread of the offences would give an insight not only into the offender's likely location but also other aspects that could lead to his apprehension, because how a serial rapist commits his crimes casts a 'shadow'. And this shadow cannot be erased because it arises from his past — which he cannot change.

We all knew that unless we changed our investigative methodology, we would continue to pull in an empty net and the Ghost would continue on his brutal journey. After further research from overseas experiences, much of which was done in what private time we had, the plan was hatched. What we needed was a method to obtain information from stored police records that would incorporate the factors we deduced that we knew about our Ghost to create a suspect list. This was a giant step back into the Ghost's past to find him there, as it seemed we could not catch him in the present. Having managed this giant task, we would then need to create prioritised suspect lists and have a large team to obtain blood from those on lists.

The plan was written up and presented to the district commander and regional commander. It stated our need for a bigger budget and staff from around the country to create a massive team to put this new approach in place. The search for the Ghost was to become the largest and longest active manhunt in New Zealand police history. Given the manpower and cost involved, there was a lot on the line for the team, and especially for John; a very courageous stand by him.

The plan was approved, but of course it took a little more time to get the extra staff from around the country and the finance in place. We now had a decent budget, along with access to night-shift uniformed staff for the covert street-observation part of the inquiry. But the key part of Operation Park was developing a profile of the offender from the geographic and behavioural theories. We were looking for the Ghost somewhere in his criminal past, as opposed to the present — which was of course a concept opposite to that of most criminal investigations that rely on the theory that the first 48 hours after a serious crime are the most crucial.

According to David Canter, marauder rapists commit their crimes in an area they know well, as they have a mental map of the possibilities the geography provides — both for committing the crime and getting away afterwards. This means they are likely to live in that area. From our map of the Ghost's intruder rapes over the years, we concluded that he lived in Ōtara in 1988 and 1989, in Mt Albert in 1991 and 1994, and in Manurewa in 1993. As was typical of this type of offender, he would have been convicted of a house burglary ten years prior to his first rape, in 1988. He was also likely to have been placed in a juvenile institution between the ages of twelve and seventeen, and to have been referred to the Department of Education's psychological services as a child. And at some point he was likely to have been identified through fingerprints, leading him to be extremely careful about leaving no fingerprints at the rape scenes.

Profiling research also suggested that between 1988 and 1994, while living in Ōtara, he would have been arrested for a variety of offences that were not sexually related. This was a surprise to all of us — why would 'convicted sexual offender' not be one of the points in our profile? But the research showed that a previous sexual conviction was not a high probability any more than shoplifting was. And in the end, when we'd caught the Ghost, this proved to be right: he had no previous sexual charges. It shows how wrong we were originally when we started looking for known sexual offenders for stranger intruder rapes; that would never have led us to the offender.

There was one more part to the profile that was intriguing. The map of the Ghost's offences revealed a triangular area in the residential part of Ōtara where he had made no attacks. According to David Canter, this meant that there was something in this area — the rapist's 'safety zone' — that was significant to him. There had to be a reason why he had not committed rapes there at any point.

Many aspects of the profile we developed were searchable. When someone is arrested, charge data is created. We record the details of the charge — type of offence, where it occurred, and when. Then there are details of the offender: race/ethnicity, age, build and height. We have their name, their address at the time of the arrest, and can link them to any previous convictions or charges. Now we had a list of searchable details of the offender, the next challenge was how to actually find him among the thousands of other people who might fall into some of these categories — the needle in the haystack. At first, we tried to use the thousands of copies of charge sheets of arrested offenders, having them checked by retired police officers. It meant a great reunion for those involved, but failed — principally due to the sheer volume of charge sheets involved. While this system had been successful in the reinvestigation of the Janine Law homicide a year earlier, the time span of the attacks we were investigating in Operation Park and the enormous number of charge sheets involved was prohibitive.

WE ALREADY HAD the National Law Enforcement Data Base — the Wanganui Computer — which had become operational around 1976. The details of all charges laid by police were entered into this computer system at the station where the transgressor had been arrested or charged, and were linked to a unique PRN — personal record number. These were the same details we had on the physical charge sheets, but because they were held in a computer there was the opportunity to access them more readily. All we needed for Operation Park was a computer program to be quickly designed so we could actually access all those details and use them to prepare prioritised suspect lists.

Fortunately, on our team we now had a computer maestro by the name of Frank van der Zwaag. Having been supported by Mitford, John Manning and Lambo to get through the internal legal and privacy hurdles, he developed a way of sourcing all the data we needed directly from the Wanganui Computer system. It was convoluted and complicated, but the results were staggering — once Frank had turned what to us was double-Dutch into a clear picture that all of us could follow.

Frank started by creating a database of suspects based on the arrest records — we were confident that this would contain the name of the offender. There were over 4600 names; an impossible number to process manually. After removing those who were either in jail or overseas at the time any of the DNA-linked rapes were committed, or were not the right ethnicity or build, Frank got the list down to just over 2500. Still a massive number.

The next step was to produce a series of suspect lists based on age (thirties), ethnicity (Māori or Pasifika), build (slim, medium height), a criminal history of burglary and addresses in the area where the crimes occurred. The first-priority lists were based on fairly tight criteria and contained less than 100 names; lists further down the hierarchy were broadened to catch more people in the net.

Fortunately for us, the offender had done us a favour by leaving a small amount of blood at one of the rape scenes in Papatoetoe. It meant that Sue and her team at ESR could eliminate samples based on blood type, which was so much quicker than DNA testing. Back then, it took at least a month to obtain a DNA profile. Detectives and uniformed staff were already busy collecting blood samples from anyone who fitted the vague description we had, or who had been nominated by some source. The priority now shifted to collecting blood from people on our suspect lists — starting with the first list and moving down. This was referred to as the 'blooding phase', after Wambaugh's book *The Blooding*. The ESR staff were about to be rushed off their feet. Dozens of detectives were involved in this phase alone. We had people from all over the North Island staying in motels in South Auckland. There was even a competition to establish who could collect the most bloods in a week. By the time I arrived at work at 7 a.m. each morning, a number of staff would already be out pulling suspects from their beds for blooding, all hoping to take blood from the Ghost.

Suspects from whom samples couldn't be taken on religious grounds, or for some other reason, could request a buccal (mouth) swab rather than a blood sample. This wasn't a problem, but it did mean that these samples could not go through the preliminary blood-type screening. Instead they proceeded directly to the much longer and more expensive DNA process. On this basis alone, it was not something we encouraged.

Despite the time it took to formulate the suspect lists and step up the operation on the ground, the blooding phase was fully up and running late in 1994 and into early 1995. Meanwhile, the rapist kept attacking. One rape in Māngere in late 1994 took place after the usual heavy rainstorm, which seemed to trigger some subconscious spark within the Ghost. When I attended the scene, the mist was lifting after the overnight rain; it was an eerie and macabre scene, like something out of an Alfred Hitchcock movie. He had set up a makeshift bed in a neighbour's backyard, using linen from the victim's house and ties for her hands and ankles, and a knife from her house was found in the fence nearby. A police dog tracked the offender across a neighbouring park, but stopped short by the side of a road. It meant that the offender was using a car and likely living in a completely different suburb. Had we frightened him out of committing his crimes in Ōtara and Manurewa?

All South Auckland residents were living in fear. The politicians were still having a field day, usually at our expense. Although politicians had been useful at the start, in getting the ball rolling, now they were taking senior staff out of the investigation daily to answer pedantic questions to fuel debate and win points in Parliament. Finally, the relentless work paid off. By now we were quite far down the lists of suspects and the net had been spread fairly wide. But in April 1995, Detective Barry Raemaki from Waitematā District had the name of the Ghost on his blooding list. After numerous attempts to obtain a blood sample, he finally took a saliva sample on 26 April.

ON 20 JUNE 1995 we got the call from Sue V at ESR: she had a 'first probe' DNA profile that matched our Ghost. He turned out to be a smallish, recently married man called Joseph Stephenson Thompson. He had not been on our first list of suspects — not because the system wasn't working, but because he was a year older than this list's maximum of 35 years. In hindsight, we should have listened to the youngest victim, the ten-year-old from Manurewa, who had placed his age at 37. From the mouths of children . . .

But it's easy to be wise in hindsight. The FBI acknowledges that predicting age is difficult, as people mature at different stages. At the time, we had to have some sort of cut-off point or the lists would have contained too many suspects to be workable. We were unlucky that Thompson's name wasn't in those early lists. But it was in the subsequent lists. Quite amazing, really, as in all the case files I had and in all the years of trying to locate the Ghost, up until that point his name had not featured once! This brought home to me the power of profiling, of finding an offender through their criminal past.

Looking at Thompson's file, it was clear that he slotted into most of the classifications. He was a perfect match for the physical description, and had been convicted for a burglary at the age of fifteen, ten years before the rapes began. He had lived in all the suburbs in our profile at all the right times: Ōtara in 1988–89, Mt Albert in 1991 and Manurewa in 1993. He was identified through fingerprints in 1985, and between 1988 and 1991 had been arrested for several non-sexual crimes in Ōtara. As an adolescent he had been in a boys' home, although had not been referred to psychological services. This last point was the only one that didn't match the profile.

As for the 'safe zone', a triangular area of residential streets in

Ōtara, this was where his parents lived, in different houses after having separated. When Thompson was living in Manurewa, he would drive to one of his parents' addresses, leave his car in their driveway and maraud out from there. The dysfunctional nature of the family meant that a car in their driveway at night did not raise any suspicions. Unfortunately, he had not given either of these addresses any time he had been charged, so the information was not in the Wanganui Computer. If it had been, it would have resulted in a much earlier identification.

By the end of Operation Park, I hardly ever met a police officer who had not at some time played some role in the operation. By now most understood the role of DNA, which certainly hadn't been the case at the beginning of the inquiry — when one senior officer made the serious suggestion that we should develop the DNA to see what the offender looked like, just as they had in the then-recent movie *Jurassic Park*. The journey, however, had been long and frustrating. From the commencement of the profiling phase to identifying the offender took about six months, including reduced staffing over Christmas. But we had learnt much, and knew that in future we could improve on the profiling process by fine-tuning our systems.

Profiling has become a well-publicised policing tool, particularly popular with the media, but (like DNA identification) it was not a well-known tool in 1994 New Zealand. This was trail-blazing at its best. Little did we know how quickly it would be required again.

We knew we had the Ghost; now we had to arrest him.

8. CATCHING THE GHOST — 'I'VE BEEN WAITING FOR YOU GUYS'

ALTHOUGH WE FINALLY KNEW THE face of the man who had terrorised South Auckland for years, eluding the police for all that time, we didn't yet have enough evidence to arrest Joseph Thompson. The DNA match was just a 'first probe', insufficient as court evidence, and a second DNA result was needed to confirm what we all knew to be the truth. This would take several more weeks.

For the Ghost to commit another attack when we knew he was our man would be unthinkable; it must not happen. A team led by Detective Sergeant Richard Middleton (son of my early boss 'Spooky' Middleton) kept Thompson under 24/7 observation for the next month. This was a huge exercise, possibly bigger than you might imagine. It involved a team rostered on twelve-hour shifts around the clock watching his house and following his movements. One constable spent every night hanging out of a tree near Thompson's home, which was still in Mt Albert. He loved the task — he'd been trained for it in the army before joining the police. Of course it was winter, which did make the task more challenging.

On one occasion Thompson went walkabout late at night after a quarrel with his wife, who left shortly afterwards. After Thompson was seen looking through the windows of a few houses, Middleton put the police helicopter up in the area and there were a number of marked police cars driving around with their blue and red lights flashing. This had the desired effect: Thompson briskly returned home, confirmed by our special army Tarzan in his tree.

Thompson's arrest was thoroughly planned during the month leading up to the event. We would need to conduct many interviews and execute search warrants across the city. His extended family, his partner, his workplace and his workmates would all be involved. Thompson was working at the Bluebird factory a mere mile from our base. We were keen to check his work locker, hoping to get hold of a pair of size 9–11 John Bull boots.

Detective Sergeant Brett Simpson — Simpo — and I were tasked with collecting Thompson and then interviewing him. To prepare us for this we went to all the scenes and met many of the victims, so that Simpo, as O/C Suspects, was fully equipped for his senior role in the interview. I knew the scenes backwards by this time, and the victims as well. One adult victim twigged that our visit meant something was happening. She asked if we knew who the rapist was, but of course we couldn't let on what was pending in a few days' time. However, I gave her a discreet wink as we left, figuring she had the right to know before the rest of New Zealand.

WHEN THE DNA confirmation from Sue at ESR came in, on Tuesday 11 July 1995, we were ready for action. By chance, this happened to be the same day that Joseph Thompson threw out his John Bull work boots. A pity, but in the end it didn't matter. You can't expect everything to fall perfectly into place the way it does in a TV crime show.

That Saturday, 15 July, was D-Day. We started very early getting teams spread out in every direction; they all had to wait until we had uplifted Thompson before they could hit their targets, but at least they'd be in place already.

Although keyed up, I was very ready for this big day. I left home before anyone else had risen, leaving a note to say I'd be very late home but not giving any further details — I always tried to keep the brutal realities of my daily work away from my family, as far as that was possible. This was particularly hard when rapes and murders hit the newspapers and TV and those realities were right there in front of them.

Simpo and I led a fleet of vehicles from the Gordon Road CIB offices in Ōtāhuhu, including dog teams in case Thompson decided to try a runner. There was a hiccup at the electric gate, which initially failed to operate. I hoped this wasn't a bad omen for the rest of the day. On the way to Mt Albert, I thought over what our reception might be, mentally running through all the possible scenarios and how we would deal with each one. At the same time apprehensive and excited, the adrenaline really began to kick in as we drew nearer to Thompson's house. I suspected he would have considered the possibility that one day the police would be knocking on his door. We knew he was home because our man in the tree had told us so.

Simpo and I knocked on that door in Mt Albert. And the Ghost,

Joe Thompson — a small-framed Māori man with a bit of a hunch in his back — opened it. Simpo told him we were the police.

'Oh yeah,' he replied, 'I've been waiting for you guys. Come in, I'll just have a wash. I'll need a jacket, too.'

We all shook hands, and Brett introduced me to Thompson.

'Oh, you're Dave Henwood?' he said. 'I was going to ring you.'

There was a gobsmacking moment of realisation: his response signified total submission. Thompson was opening the door not only to his home but also into his life. We would have been idiots to close it in his face by immediately throwing him in cuffs and dragging him across the road to the car. Reading the moment, both Simpo and I instinctively knew what to do. We needed to build on this initial friendly atmosphere. I knew from experience that if we managed to keep it going, we would extract a clear and complete story from Thompson. In order to get the result we needed, neither Brett nor I revealed our internal responses — at least, we tried not to. Inwardly in disbelief at Thompson's affable response, Simpo asked him if he knew why we were there.

'Yeah, it had to come, I know that,' he replied. He made it clear to us he would be open and frank about all that he had done. To confirm this, we drove past the house in Papatoetoe where I had given the victim a discreet wink. Thompson immediately pointed to it and said that 'a Pākehā lady' lived there.

In the end, it was to be that easy; almost an anti-climax. We provided Thompson with everything required by the Bill of Rights Act. He refused a solicitor. During the interview, which we captured on video, he sat opposite Simpo in a white T-shirt and baseball cap with his arms folded, seeming relaxed. This was made possible by the friendly atmosphere Simpo and I had created in this little cubicle interview room. We had made it a safe place where Thompson could tell all to his 'two new friends'.

I sat to the side, gripping my complainants' file notes. *This* was the man who had terrorised women for almost twelve years. Surreal. I was noting down some of Thompson's responses that I thought were important at the time, but after a while, as the interview went on, I stopped this and simply listened.

The level of detail and accuracy Thompson provided about every rape was astounding. It was also totally credible. He went from crime to crime, opening up to us his sex-crime world from start to finish. We would show him a photo of an address and he would then describe how he had gained access to the house, provide a description of the victim, a description of the offence and, on occasion, would recall when the offence had taken place.

The rapes he described included all but three on my list of 44. One of these three had been a DNA hit but for some reason he could not recall it. This was odd, considering his remarkable recall of all the others. The other two were attacks that hadn't resulted in rape, which may have clouded his memory. One would be cleared up later with a written explanation from Thompson, leaving just one on our list that we could not link him to. In this attack, the offender had entered the room but had been disturbed early, before the sexual assault was even commenced, and therefore Thompson's characteristic sexual behaviours had not been evident. Either he had not committed this offence, or it had not registered sufficiently in his memory. As there was no DNA and no confession, he was not charged with this attack.

On the following day, a Sunday, we continued the interview. We took Thompson for a drive around Auckland's central suburbs and the well-trodden streets of South Auckland. He pointed out the houses where he had attacked women. His clarity of memory about each was unbelievably accurate, both in the description of the attack, the mode of entry to the house, and the description of the victim. They went back to his first attack twelve years earlier in Mt Eden. Research shows that this isn't unusual — the reason for serial rapists' clear memories of their offences is that they relive the incident over and over in their mind, reinforcing it so that it becomes a vivid memory and (in some cases) a masturbatory aid.

What we were listening to was Thompson's life being relayed from his perspective. The victims he referred to seemed to be just numbers to him. Did he feel any remorse? At the time of the interview we didn't want to interrupt the flow and kill the 'friendship' by bringing up the subject of remorse; it was not the right time.

When we finally emerged from the interview room, it was as if a bond had been created between the three of us. This little interview room had been our place with Thompson for twenty-plus hours together, play-acting — on our part — a game of friendship and understanding. We tried to cover up any personal feelings of revulsion, both in the interview room and afterwards. We kept Thompson as our 'friend' until sentencing was over, and then just dropped him off at Pāremoremo prison and walked away.

After the interview was over, we accompanied Thompson to the cells and made it clear to the custody officer that he was a suicide risk — and that he was to stay alive for his court appearance on Monday. There had in fact been no indication that he was a suicide risk, but we did not want to make assumptions.

It was not until a few days after the interview that I was able to rationalise what we had heard, and to match the descriptions of each of the rapes and attacks to specific victims. In the small interview room it was like we were playing a role on stage in order to draw out the full performance from 'our friend Joe'. But afterwards I had to slip out of that character and back into reality. And what a reality it was!

More than twenty hours of video interview finished with an uninterrupted monologue from Thompson, explaining his actions. He told us that he had become a sexual abuser because of 'a vicious cycle that goes around and around'; he was just part of that cycle. He claimed that he had been abused as a child and had become conditioned to those kind of things. Excerpts from the transcript of our interview gives some insight into what drove his offending.

> I get this urge like getting hungry for a feed. I don't know
> if it is sex or whether it is to have somebody in my arms,
> whether it is love, whether it is hate. I get this compulsion to
> go out and do these things and I find when I am out there
> doing it, I can't stop and I can't let anybody stop me doing it.
> I feel remorse and guilt and I feel shit afterwards and then
> suddenly I get this urge again and then I push all that shit
> aside and I go out and do it again.

He blamed the physical abuse he experienced as a child for making him incapable of satisfying an adult woman. According to his logic, the only way he could achieve sexual gratification was to 'have somebody young', though he claimed that he had never been satisfied with what he was doing.

Thompson also claimed to have caught a lot of diseases from all the people he attacked, and that changed his body. This comment made me cringe — inwardly — more than any other he made. It showed what a narcissistic, self-centred bastard he was. To my knowledge, he never used a condom at any of the rape scenes.

This worked out well for us, as he never took any care regarding leaving DNA evidence. Less so for his victims, though — after undergoing medical examinations and tests, some of them learnt they had contracted chlamydia.

THE STYLE OF our interviewing was very open-ended, with little interruption from either of us. Later, we received some criticism from a few police staff who saw the videoed interview — or part of it — suggesting that we had not taken sufficient control of the interview room, leaving Thompson in control. But why would we try to control it when we were getting exactly what we needed from him without this? We deliberately kept the questions open-ended because by now we were aware that Thompson would say anything if he thought it would please us. This was why we also asked him about some rapes that we knew he hadn't carried out — to check that he was not admitting to every sex crime from Jack the Ripper onwards. We had to be sure that what we were getting from him was the truth. By testing him like this, we knew we were.

There were occasions when some of his answers or statements needed an explanation. If Simpo didn't pick up on it, then I would. When it became clear that we were getting a total confession, in detail, of every crime he had committed — including a lot of rapes we didn't know about — I was intrigued to know his motivation. I asked him questions about why the rapes had taken place on wet nights — what were the triggers? — but I don't think Thompson really knew. He tried to provide us with an explanation, but he was clearly grasping at straws and trying to please. He didn't even seem to realise that most of his rapes had taken place on wet nights.

During the long interview sessions I also took a little time out of the rape admissions to clarify other details. One was the glue-sniffer who had placed a chair under the window of Thompson's youngest victim, the ten-year-old girl in Manurewa. Another was a coat that had been left behind at the eerie Hitchcock-like rape scene in Māngere in late 1994.

The coat, which we had done so much investigation work on, believing it to be the offender's, turned out to belong to the victim of that rape. It had been taken from her address by Thompson. This was galling. We had sourced his semen (and therefore his DNA) from many scenes, along with his blood at Papatoetoe, and there were those John Bull boot impressions at many scenes — but the coat was the first item we could actually touch that we believed he had left behind. Many hours of forensic work went into this coat in the hope that it would lead us to the offender. We also took it to the Ōtara market a number of times to see if anyone would recognise it. But nothing.

We likewise spent many hours trying to locate the two glue-sniffers, eventually realising that even if we had identified them, they would not have led us to Thompson. During the interview, Thompson told us he'd been sitting under a tree across the road, keeping relatively dry in the pouring rain, while watching the glue-sniffers. When they left, he entered the house using the chair they had so conveniently placed under the window. Windows were a common entry point for the Ghost, so the glue-sniffers had unintentionally assisted him in committing this heinous, appalling crime. Thompson had also spotted the two witnesses on the railway bridge, so waited for them to move away before entering the victim's home and abducting her. This incident clearly showed how aware Thompson was of his environment and how practised he was at stalking his victims in the hours of darkness.

Not surprisingly, Thompson admitted to a lot of rapes we didn't know about — either because they had not been reported to the police, or because they were files we had never found. Both in South Auckland and the central suburbs there were some police files that had become lost in a filing system that did not provide any easy way to locate unsolved or solved rapes of a specific type, such as 'stranger intruder' rapes like Thompson's. You could find files by complainant's name (meaning the victim), or offender name, or location. Although the files were coded, this wasn't comprehensive enough. Some were coded under a different offence; also, the coding did not identify attempted rapes, or stranger attacks that might not have been considered sexually motivated. We were looking for stranger attacks with sexual motivation. I struggled with and tried to fix this filing problem right up to the time I retired.

The only way we could find historical rape cases hidden within the filing system was to encourage older detectives to come forward. From them we would obtain details of any rapes or sexual attacks they might have attended, including offender names or, if unsolved, complainant names. Of course, once Thompson had confessed and pointed out a rape scene, we could locate the file — if it had been reported. Later, after the profiling unit had been set up, the file of any unsolved rape was retained there and visible in our records system. From this point onwards, no rape file that we recovered from the filing system was ever returned; many remained open at the profiling unit for years. One particular file, that was at a glance clearly not related to Thompson's offences, was for a rape committed in Panmure. This was held in the Operation Park office at Manukau and later became an important component of Operation Harvey, the major investigation that was to follow.

Importantly, Thompson did not admit to any of the rapes

that I had eliminated due to having a clearly different modus operandi and signature behaviour. Modus operandi, or MO, is a learnt behaviour around what the offender does to commit the crime and also prevent himself from being caught. This may alter as his criminal career progresses and he learns from his mistakes. A sex offender's signature relates to the ritual behaviours that he (it is usually a 'he') carries out in order to satisfy himself. This was important to me both then and later. It showed me that if you looked closely enough, and understood the behaviour of an offender in a series of stranger rapes, it was possible to identify those crimes for which he was responsible and to eliminate those for which he was *not* responsible.

JOSEPH THOMPSON FRONTED court on Monday 17 July 1995. He was defended by Kevin Ryan QC, who was professional as always — but on a hiding to nothing with this case. Thompson was remanded to the Mason Clinic, a specialist mental health service, for a psychiatric assessment. He returned to court two weeks later to plead guilty to all of the 129 charges on the massive indictment — the largest ever number of charges on an indictment in a court in a Commonwealth country at the time.

Simpo and I had brought Thompson to court to hear the charges. We stood alongside him for what felt like a lifetime while he pleaded guilty — individually — to each and every one of the charges. From memory, there were over 70 individual incidents, including incest, that Thompson admitted to. He was charged with 50 of these. His early guilty plea prevented a full investigation into the remainder — we just could not get them ready in time for his sentencing hearing. This included the incest charges, despite

Thompson having made a comment, during the interview, about the cycle of abuse: 'I even did it to my own children.' He was not charged with any offences against his children or his nieces. For some other cases, we had as yet no complaint. We did take Thompson out over a few days to point out other offences, although it was obviously too late to charge him with these. Some victims refused to reveal any details of the attacks on them, and some denied ever being attacked. Each woman will have had her reasons, and we had to respect these.

The two weeks between Thompson's guilty plea and his sentencing were very busy. We prepared victim-impact reports, a 'summary of facts', a large pictorial chart outlining all the dates, scenes, complainants, locations, CRNs (court record numbers), property stolen, entry style, type of offence, and much more. The 'summary of facts' (which outlined each offence in detail individually for the 50 victims) along with the victim-impact reports filled three A4 box-type folders. All of this was used at his sentencing.

I had drafted the pictorial chart, which was expertly made printable in computer format and then printed out very large by Frank with Lambo's assistance. I was not very adept with technology at the time. This chart, printed on heavy-duty paper that had been coated with plastic, was on the wall above Justice Fisher when he sentenced Joseph Thompson. It fell from the wall at one point during the long sentencing, almost landing on Justice Fisher's head.

The crown prosecutor was Simon Moore, whom I had dealt with many times previously. The quality of his two-hour sentencing address was what we had come to expect from this compelling advocate for the Crown over many years in courts in central and south Auckland.

Kevin Ryan, acting for the defence, started by complimenting the police investigation, which he described as one of the most diligent he had encountered in his 39-year career. I viewed this as a direct attack on the criticism of police by politicians in the lead-up to Thompson's arrest. Regardless of anything Kevin had to say, though, the significance and number of Thompson's crimes meant that he was only ever going to receive the severest of sentencing. The early guilty plea did perhaps have some influence — if he had not done this, would have led to a trial that would have been a horrendous and harrowing affair for everyone concerned, particularly the victims. In hindsight, a trial would also have had an impact on Operation Harvey, which followed directly on the tail of Park. These early guilty pleas by Thompson were appreciated by everyone involved — these, together with his open confession, were his only saving graces. Given that young girls made up a large number of the 50 victims, putting them through the experience of a trial would have been a nightmare. There might even have been more than one trial and they could have dragged on for years, causing further misery for everyone.

Thompson received a sentence of 30 years in prison, with 25 years before he could apply for parole. At that time this was the longest sentence ever imposed in New Zealand and the most severe sentence since the abolition of capital punishment in this country. As Justice Fisher said at Thompson's sentencing, 'It is difficult to think of any person who has brought more pain and misery to so many people in New Zealand history.'

While everyone else involved in the investigation was celebrating at the Howick Club, Simpo and I were dropping Thompson off at Pāremoremo prison for the final time. Thompson did not want us, two officers he had come to consider his friends, to go. We drove around for a bit while he pointed out further attack locations, and he made a number of comments that aligned perfectly with what we had now learnt about the young Joe. His records with child welfare and the boys' home recorded him as always trying to stay friendly with anyone in authority. While at the boys' home, he was an excellent student. He liked the environment, with its safe walls and line-in-the-sand boundaries that he had never experienced at home. Prison gave the same feeling to Thompson — security; he hinted that he recognised this in himself. It hardly seemed to be a punishment, given that being incarcerated represented security to him. Thompson was still doing it his way. I believed the IQ test he had completed at the Mason Clinic, which showed that he was well above average in intelligence.

His last words to us were, perhaps surprisingly, to thank us. 'I'm actually glad that this happened,' he said to me. 'I'm glad it's you two, you and Brett, that have been the ones that have been with me ever since. To me, the police were just police, and I didn't think there was a human side to police, an understanding side. I realise I've been wrong about the police for a long time. I just want to say thanks to you guys, eh, it's been a lot of pain for me all my life.'

While this type of relationship between police and offender is not unusual, I don't think it is believed outside of police circles. While Joseph Thompson is an extreme case because of his personality and his keenness to get on well with authority, the same sort of thing has been my experience in many cases throughout my career.

Leaving the prison, we arrived at the celebrations in time for a photograph with a large group that included district commanders and the commissioner. I think the only ones missing from the photograph were the nurses who actually took the blood from the many suspects. I had a drink and a few words with colleagues before wandering home, wondering what would come next. I knew that whatever it was would be a step down after this marathon hunt for the Ghost. Hopefully it would also involve less overtime.

WE DID HEAR from Thompson once more after this. He wrote to acknowledge one of the three crimes he had claimed not to have remembered during our initial interview. He wanted to have it all finished with, and not leave one matter sticking in his craw as he wasted away his days and nights in his structured, controlled home in Pāremoremo maximum-security prison. The wording of the letter provided an insight into how Thompson's mind worked. Still wanting to impress his new mates, he used police parlance:

> This is to verify that I, Joseph Stephenson Thompson, born 3 August 1958, residing at Auckland prison Paremoremo admit and accept that it was I who on the night of the 23 February 1989 proceeded to break and enter the said address being [deleted], Ōtara. My intention was that of rape and while I was in the building, I encountered a woman who was sleeping. She was alone in the house. When I attempted to rape her, she immediately awoke and called out 'Jesus loves you'.
>
> I quickly found I was not able to overcome her. She was very frantic in her efforts to dissuade my intentions and kept yelling 'Jesus loves you'. I thought her to be a Māori or Polynesian woman between the age of 22–26 years old. I quickly left her home and ran off up the road. All credit to Jesus.

Not bad for someone who had very little schooling past inter-mediate, and not much before that. But more than this, it highlights how much knowledge about police jargon, facts and systems an interviewee picks up during the interview process. This would become an important lesson for later.

That aside, if you read Thompson's monologues carefully, you notice that something crucial is missing. He talks a lot about himself and how it all affected *him*. The personal pronoun 'I' is repeated over and over. As a psychologist once said to me about someone similar, 'his "Is" are too close together'. Not a word of concern about the impact of his crime on his victims, or how sorry he was for what he did to them and how he ruined their lives. He focused on how he 'caught a lot of diseases' from the women he raped, while the truth was that *he* was passing STDs on to his victims.

He had no concept of the magnitude of what he had done; how he had damaged the lives of as many as 70 women and girls forever. Many young girls will live with the trauma of their dreadful experience their entire lives — and let's not forget the suffering of their families. Thompson's heart-breaking legacy, one that he consistently failed to recognise and acknowledge, was that he robbed girls of their childhoods, gave them insomnia, eating disorders, terror and paranoia, and turned some of them towards alcohol and crime. Some girls and women had lasting physical injuries. Others had their marital relationships destroyed; yet others had their family relationships and friendships shattered. Some moved homes, leaving Auckland. I am aware that one of his young rape victims later committed suicide.

Thompson thought a lot about *his* life and *his* troubles. He was self-absorbed, and disconnected not only from his victims but also from anyone else. Even if he tried to make out that he was a 'truly repentant man who had found God' — really? Although he was with the Jehovah's Witnesses and used this as a reason to initially refuse a blood test, they don't actually have a rule about that. It was self-serving. He would always be thinking about what to do next, not — hell, what have I done to all those girls and women? He will probably spend the rest of his time on earth thinking about his life from a prison cell, the place where he is most comfortable, not sparing a thought to the wreckage he left behind — a wreckage that others have been left to manage.

Dr Heinz Albrecht, the psychiatrist who examined Thompson, thought that he was a 'typical serial offender' whose psychological problems had developed because of the sexual abuse he suffered as a child. For all of us, according to Dr Albrecht, life is a puzzle — but Thompson started out with a warped frame, distorted by the abuse, and some pieces of his puzzle simply refused to fit. Like a child using a fist to bang a piece of puzzle into a space not meant for it, Thompson became angry at the mismatch between the behaviour expected by society and that he was experiencing at home. Not only abused, but also seemingly unwanted, as he, and many of his siblings, were sent away to live with various relatives and then the boys' home.

Despite his attempts to be friendly with those in authority, Thompson learnt not to trust anyone. There was no one he could talk to. Clearly intelligent, he spent much time thinking about this world of his that was so miserable, wondering how to overcome his background — but was unable to do so. Irritability would give way to anger, frequent use of drugs and alcohol, and long walks, day after day and into the night. Feelings of hatred, first towards his family and then towards others, began to develop, along with the sense of not being in control.

Joseph Thompson's rapes were not about the sex, but an attempt to solve his problems through violence, following the model he had been shown as a child. But, of course, it didn't work, so he kept trying, hoping for a better result each time — and so became a serial rapist. As Dr Albrecht said, quoted in *Caught by his Past* by Jan Corbett:

> Serial offenders don't kill at the beginning. They seek sex,
> then control, then they rape and then they kill. He would
> have graduated to the ultimate type of control; he would have
> killed. That is where Mr Thompson was heading.

Dr Albrecht's compelling analysis certainly fitted perfectly to the Thompson I knew from the investigation files and the twenty hours of interviewing. It led me to much reading on the subject and drew me deeper into this area of the psychology of rapists. It propelled me into the next period of my policing life, which — not by chance — fell into the same area of profiling, behavioural analysis, and investigating and understanding serial rapists through their displayed behaviour during their offending.

While Thompson's life story gives a clear picture of how innate personality and the life journey join forces to produce a monster, it is worth noting that many people are brought up in similar neglectful abandonment and experience a disgustingly depraved home life but do not become serial rapists. Some turn out to be bad criminals of another type, but others manage to spring clear of the muck that represented their childhood to become of great benefit to society. In Thompson's case, however, hundreds of innocent people paid the penalty for the internal conflict produced by the shameful neglect of Thompson by his parents coupled with his narcissistic personality.

Thompson appealed his sentence and the minimum parole period; it was rejected. He became eligible to apply for parole in 2020 but, not unexpectedly, remains in prison. At his 2023 hearing, the parole board concluded that despite some interest in rehabilitation programmes, he remained an undue risk. At the time of writing, his next parole hearing is due in 2025. However, the Ghost is likely to remain in prison for some time yet.

IT WAS THE end of two and a half years of pursuing this one man. What followed for me was putting the massive Park file to bed. This took a month or so, sitting in the office at Manukau sorting through almost a hundred box-style folders. It involved disposing of exhibits, both written notes and physical items, not required to be archived.

This task placed me in the same office and in close company with those involved in a new investigation, named Operation Harvey. It was another serial rape case and involved many of the key staff from Operation Park, including Mitford, Lambo and Frank. The operation covered a number of rapes in South Auckland from the late 1980s, as well as one in Hillsborough, one in Rotorua in 1989, and the rape and murder of 39-year-old Susan Burdett in 1992. The investigating strategy mirrored that of Operation Park. The team was not as large as the Park team but was still substantial, and also included a blooding team operating out of Rotorua because of the case there. The investigation was led by an old mate, 'Ruthers' — now Detective Inspector Steve Rutherford — who'd been a squad supervisor of mine from the early days of working in CIB. He had also led the successful reinvestigation of the Janine Law case and many other notorious homicide investigations.

I found this all very interesting, and could not help but get some idea what the case was about during lunchtime discussions with Mitford and Lambo. But I was not on the team. John Manning, who had been helping Auckland Central with yet another rape series, code-named Atlas, had recently been assigned to other duties. He suggested that I be seconded to Operation Atlas to apply the skills I had developed both during and since Operation Park: the linking of crimes to other crimes, and of crimes to single offenders, through behavioural analysis of rapists. I was very eager to take on this challenge — it meant I would not be returning to routine work after Operation Park. My appetite for furthering my experience and continuing my journey into the close study of rape behaviour had been fired up by Park. This was my opportunity to dig even deeper.

9. THE HUNT FOR THE LONE WOLF

SO IT WAS THAT I found myself at Auckland Central police station at the beginning of 1996, reviewing rape case files as part of Operation Atlas. Twenty-six years had passed since I had arrived at Trentham to start my police training. I was 43 years old and by now had six children.

The rapes being investigated in Operation Atlas had commenced in November 1995 with a number of attacks in the central suburbs of Auckland, at least some of which were believed to be the work of one serial offender. Central wanted to know if this was correct. My role was to use behavioural analysis to link the files that belonged to an exclusive offender and eliminate any that, in my view, did not belong.

Interestingly, during Operation Park a certain politician had suggested that the police had not allocated many staff to the inquiry because most of the victims were Māori and Pasifika and lived in the low socioeconomic areas of South Auckland. This was untrue. It was simply due to a lack of police staff and resources; this type of inquiry is staff-intensive. Operation Atlas was at the other end of the affluence scale, focusing on rapes taking place in the medium-to-high socioeconomic suburbs of Ponsonby, Mt Eden, St Marys Bay and Remuera, which generally involved Pākehā women — yet the staffing issues were similar to Park. Despite being in the largest police district in the country, by the numbers, anyway, staff resourcing remained an ongoing issue for the officer-in-charge, even after the massive inquiry that was Operation Park — which should have opened the eyes of everyone involved to the nature of serial rape investigations and what they required.

Police results and, subsequently, budgets, were measured by statistics, which were at best unreliable and could be skewed at will. The police hierarchy was, of course, accountable to the politicians who measured progress by these statistics. Like a battle, it fell to the soldiers in the trenches to make the difference. Our battleground ethos was to help individual victims in the best way we could. Those battle-weary detectives and other staff still at the coalface know best how to make things work and bring those responsible for crimes to task. Most police at the coalface want the same outcome.

As Operation Park had shown, to catch serial rapists we needed both sufficient staff to work on the investigation *and* the right methodology. I started reviewing files following the same methodology I had applied in Operation Park. It was an area of investigation with which I was becoming increasingly comfortable, and I felt that my knowledge and confidence were increasing. Personal interest coupled with the need to accomplish results for the victims as well as ourselves drove me to read as much as I could fit in around the travel from home to Auckland Central (and back) each day, helping with the children, and tending 2 acres of land and a large rose garden.

My review of the police files centred on complainant statements, scene documents and scene visits, analysing the information in terms of specific ritualistic behaviour, often referred to as the rapist's signature, and general/common behaviour, or modus operandi, the learnt behaviour of the offender that he practises in order to carry out his crimes and which can change throughout his career. To a degree, it is determined by victim reactions and the requirements of the crime environment.

In the Atlas rapes, all the victims were of small build, and aged 20 to 40 years. They came from professional middle-socioeconomic backgrounds, lived in suburbs that were near to each other, of similar character and with similar types of home. The attacks appeared to be premeditated and indicated knowledge of the area. They were stranger attacks that took place during the hours of darkness, with the lone intruder using a 'blitz surprise attack' style. He used no weapon, but commonly would say, 'Shut up, shut up!' He used violence purely to control the victim. The initial assault involved physical force to the area around the throat and head. Victims were gagged and their hands were tied behind their back.

The description of the offender provided by the victims, albeit unspecific, was generally consistent: muscular, of medium build, 167 to 175 centimetres in height. He had not been drinking. Because he wore gloves, there were no fingerprints found, and neither was any semen located.

The ritualistic aspects of a rape are static — unlikely to change over time or between attacks — because they are intended to satisfy the drive or fantasy needs of a particular offender. For this reason, ritualistic behaviour leads to the strongest links between crimes. Put crudely, it is whatever the offender needs to do to get his rocks off. For Atlas, the ritualistic or signature behaviours included erectile dysfunction (hence no semen at the scenes); the way the victim was moved and placed, with her upper body covered and lower body naked from the waist down, and the shining of a torch on her genitals.

An important part of criminal behavioural analysis is identifying ritualistic behaviours that are commonly observed or expected to be present, but in fact are not. In this series of rapes, one striking absence was the lack of victim participation to overcome the erectile dysfunction. Commonly, if an attacker is unable to obtain an erection he involves the victims by forcing them to perform fellatio, masturbation, or by some other type of physical or verbal contact. In these attacks this did not happen — no conversation at all, barring the initial threats designed to gain control; no violence once the victim had been tied up; no kissing or other physical stimulation; leaving the victim alone to wander around the house while she wondered whether he had left (he hadn't). It all emphasised the offender's intention to use his victims as a prop for his offending and not to involve them in any way — physically, verbally or psychologically — in his sexual performance. They were just there for him to use, for him to display his control over them and the power to do exactly as he wished. I found this to be unusual when compared with other offenders with similar erectile dysfunction.

Using this behavioural data, I linked five cases that I considered had been committed by the same offender, and thus fell under the umbrella of Operation Atlas; one further such attack occurred while I was completing my analysis. The rapes started in Sandringham in November 1995, and continued in December the same year at One Tree Hill, Remuera and Mt Eden. These were followed by an attack in Ponsonby in January 1996, and another of that year in Mt Eden late in March. I eliminated a number of others that did not fit the profile.

As we had experienced with Operation Park, the police filing system was an impediment to efficiency and we had to locate offences using alternative methods. These included searching through the crime squad book, which outlines serious events attended by crime car staff in the relevant areas. Any rapes or attempted rapes in the Auckland Central district should show up there. As a back-up, we checked through the ESR report forms (duplicates of forms sent to the ESR), which were used for most, if not all, rapes and serious attacks. These detailed any forensic exhibits along with a brief summary. Stranger intruder rapes usually had some forensic evidence that would be sent to ESR accompanied by this form.

However, neither of these approaches uncovered any further attacks over the preceding couple of years that matched the Operation Atlas offences. As with Park, we knew it was highly unlikely that this offender had just dropped in from outer space; there had to be more cases to find. And I knew where to look — Operation Harvey.

FOUR YEARS BEFORE I began my work in Operation Atlas, a woman named Susan Burdett was murdered in her home in Papatoetoe, on 23 March 1992. She had been beaten to death on her bed with a baseball bat she kept for her own protection. She had also been raped. Teenager Teina Pora made a damning confession to involvement in the rape and murder and was convicted in 1994, but police continued looking for other offenders involved in a string of rapes that included this one.

Operation Harvey was set up late in 1995 after the new DNA testing that had become available linked the murder of Susan Burdett to several stranger intruder rapes. The operation was named in memory of Mark Harvey Ennor, a detective who had worked on the original homicide investigation. He had, tragically, died in a kayaking accident in Hawke's Bay a short time after Teina Pora's conviction.

The Operation Harvey files linked by DNA started in December 1988, in Rotorua, followed by one in Ōtāhuhu in April 1989. Then, another rape in December 1991 in Hillsborough. The next was the Susan Burdett homicide, in Papatoetoe in March 1992, followed by another rape in Ōtāhuhu, in April 1992. A sixth rape was not DNA-linked, but it had occurred across the road from the 1989 Ōtāhuhu rape and took place almost exactly one year afterwards.

Six attacks, then no more. They just stopped, and it seemed there were no more for the next four years. This made no sense unless the offender was in prison, had left the country, or died. Of course all these options had been already checked by Detective Inspector Rutherford's team — another lesson from Operation Park.

Having obtained permission from Ruthers, I left Auckland Central and returned to the old Operation Park office in Manukau to analyse the Operation Harvey files. Not only was I keen to do this work, but it was a shorter daily trip from home. When I analysed these six files, enough of the same behavioural features were present for me to conclude that the Operation Harvey rapist had *not* stopped in 1992. He was, instead, continuing in 1996 in what had become the Operation Atlas rape series. We had another ghost; this time I got to call him the 'Lone Wolf'.

In police work, linkage blindness refers to a failure to consider and investigate the possibility that two series, or even two stranger rapes or sexual murders, are connected. Internationally, this failure has led to two and sometimes three separate investigations trying to solve a crime based only on the evidence available in that one crime, with embarrassing results. By *not* considering the possibility that other crimes have been committed by the same offender in neighbouring police districts, cities or states, the evidence potentially available is immediately more than halved. Conversely, when more than one rape is attributed to a single offender it exponentially increases investigative ability and is therefore a massive step towards identifying him. Linkage blindness is, naturally, less common in a small country like New Zealand with one national police department, but it still happens. Prior to Operation Park, the Joseph Thompson rapes had been a sad example of the failure to link cases in the 1980s and early 1990s to recent ones.

I brought my findings to both the Harvey and the Atlas series higher-ups. Both teams accepted that — based on my behavioural analysis — it was likely that the two series of rapes were linked to the same offender. However, the decision was made that the two should be linked forensically before officially being merged; in the meantime, they would remain separate investigations. Merging the investigations at this point would create a massive media circus and become an unnecessary distraction for the investigators.

We did not have to wait very long for the link to be confirmed. I was sure that the same offender, the Lone Wolf, had committed the Harvey series of rapes that commenced in 1988 and concluded in 1992, and the Atlas series starting in November 1995 and ongoing. So, I searched for all the unsolved intruder rapes in the greater Auckland area from before 1988 until November 1995.

The aim was to find stranger intruder sexual assault cases with the behavioural signature of the offender profile I'd developed. This would link the Atlas and Harvey series together geographically and chronologically, and would also fill the three-year gap between the two rape series.

The cases were there. Using criteria from the profile, I linked a further eight cases that occurred between 1989 and 1995, while at the same time eliminating many others that did not fit the Lone Wolf's signature. These attacks were scattered all over Auckland.

IN MAY 1996, we had three important breakthroughs that brought the hunt quickly to an arrest.

First, the last rape in the Atlas series, in Mt Eden in 1996, turned up a very small sample of semen on a bathrobe tie that was linked to the Lone Wolf. While this DNA result was not as definitive as the Harvey DNA-linked samples, it was still enough, coupled with the behavioural link, to bring the two series together under the umbrella of Operation Harvey and conclude Operation Atlas.

This pleased me: it made it clear to any doubters that my behavioural linking was accurate and one rapist was responsible for all the cases. Operating under one case umbrella also brought us all together in Manukau as one team. The investigation was complicated enough without having to work from two bases and with two different teams hunting for the same offender.

The second breakthrough was an unsuccessful attack in Epsom, right on the border with Newmarket, on a girl who was walking her dog along the street. The offender fled, but was seen to get into a vehicle connected to a Malcolm Rewa.

Finally, the reason that this was of especial interest to us was that Detective Sergeant Mark Williams, the file manager for Operation Harvey, had located a rape in Panmure, close to the border with Glen Innes, that I'd left open after Operation Park. I had immediately dismissed it as not being a Joe Thompson rape, but as we had all realised by now that finding rape files was not an easy task, it was not put back into filing. There was already talk of creating some sort of rape squad, and we'd need these files for that.

In this Panmure rape, which occurred late in December 1987, Malcolm Rewa had been identified as a suspect. To be frank, the complaint had been poorly investigated initially and this was acknowledged later in an Independent Police Conduct Authority (IPCA) inquiry. This was, of course, not the fault of Operation Harvey staff, who took some flak for it, but of those who had investigated the rape back in 1988. This file had behavioural commonalities with the others I'd identified and joined my ever-increasing list.

Subsequent inquiries into Malcolm Rewa provided connections between him and Rotorua, as well as the suburbs and immediate environs of many of the linked attacks on my list, including the Susan Burdett homicide. It was also discovered that he had a 'wanted to interview' alert for an attack in Ponsonby in early 1995, right in the middle of the Operation Atlas zone (more on this later). Of further note was that Rewa had a sexual assault conviction from the late 1970s, as well as many burglary convictions. This was all very compelling: it made him a strong suspect. But the police idiom 'Suspicion plus suspicion equals suspicion' had been around for many years, for good reason. Lots of different reasons to suspect someone does not equal proof.

Rewa's name was on the criminal profile priority suspect list that was the central focus of the suspect team. However, he had not yet been located for the purposes of obtaining a blood sample. Following the unsuccessful attack in Epsom, blood was obtained from his family members instead, and DNA testing confirmed Rewa as the Lone Wolf.

In my view, interestingly, the attack in Epsom was a spontaneous attack while all the previous ones had been planned. This was the main reason why Rewa was directly linked to it. Many serial sexual offenders, Rewa included, end up on a slippery slope and start to unwind. They become foolhardy, flagrant and lose control, making mistakes that inevitably lead to them being caught. Often they have begun to believe that they cannot be caught, which can lead to an escalation in their offending. Rewa's criminal history certainly painted him as a narcissistic personality, so it was likely he would have slipped into such feelings of invincibility.

Rewa was now presenting as a rapist who was potentially spiralling out of control — and therefore unpredictable and likely to commit offences more frequently. He was (preliminarily) linked to many intruder rapes involving violence, as well as a very brutal stranger killing (of Susan Burdett), so we knew what he was capable of. Together with other core staff, Ruthers urgently organised an arrest plan to take him out. This was executed on 13 May 1996.

ALONG WITH DETECTIVE Sergeant Karl Wright-St Clair, O/C Suspects, I had been tasked with arresting and interviewing Rewa — just as I had with Brett Simpson a year earlier in Operation Park with Joseph Thompson. Exactly the same way as before, because I knew the files and behaviour while Karl was O/C Suspects — the officer traditionally in charge of the arrest and interview.

Rewa was located at an address in Māngere late at night. The house was surrounded by members of the Armed Offenders Squad (AOS) who would then storm the house. Karl and I were waiting across the street, with bated breath, for the action to begin. The quiet suburban street suddenly exploded into action as Rewa burst out the front door, wrapped in a towel with an AOS dog hanging on to his behind and an AOS handgun up against his nostrils.

Rewa's run was over, but Karl's and mine was just beginning. We knew, from Rewa's history, that this wouldn't be a Joe Thompson-style tell-all interview. Our hope was that with a dog bite on his rear and the end in sight, a little window of opportunity might exist for Rewa to open up while at this low point in his life.

After we got him back to the Gordon Road Ōtāhuhu CIB office and took him to the interview room, we called the doctor. Meanwhile, Karl began asking Rewa questions. But it was clear from the get-go that he wouldn't be answering any. Even his name didn't seem to be an easy question for him to answer. When he was asked to provide a sample of blood, he made the point that there was plenty on the floor and to help ourselves.

The doctor arrived. Confronted with a bleeding man wrapped in a towel, looking menacing and angry, he dealt with Rewa's wounds while ensuring that he stayed as far away from the bleeding, simmering patient as possible. I sensed that the doctor considered a volcanic eruption was not far away and he didn't want to be present when it happened. Rewa had a strong muscular build and was clearly proud of his physical strength. The expression in his eyes spelled danger. I knew right then that this interview would not last long.

When it was obvious to me that Rewa would answer no questions, I asked him a few that I thought needed to be asked even if he refused to answer them.

Question one: 'Do you know Teina Pora?'

'No.'

Question two: 'Did you read about Teina Pora being charged with and convicted of the Burdett homicide?'

'Yeah.'

Question three: 'You don't know him?'

'Never met him. I'm not saying any more.'

So ended this very brief interview with a serial rapist and murderer. He told the truth about two things, though. First, there was plenty of blood on the floor of that interview room and it did not belong to Karl, the doctor or me. Second, he did not know Teina Pora. The significance of this will become clear later.

Rewa did ask to speak to Ruthers, to whom he had indicated that, maybe at the end of all this, he might fill in the final chapter. Ruthers was no novice, and knew this was unlikely to ever happen. He was right, of course.

THE ARREST HAD been the easy part; now the real work began. We had to evaluate how many of the cases on my list would provide enough evidence to put before a court. Everyone knew this was not going to be over in a month with over a hundred guilty pleas, as Operation Park had been. In May 1996 Rewa might have been a bleeding, defeated man, but he had plenty of time to catch his wind, in his corner, before the final battle commenced. And we all knew he would come out fighting — it was something he had done all his life. He thrived on confrontation, especially with authority.

A range of avenues of inquiry were commenced at this point by a large team. I was involved in only one of them: my task was to work through the files I already had and also search for more with the right behavioural links so that we could make a final count of those cases we could add to the indictment against Malcolm Rewa, the Lone Wolf.

Because of the last attack, on that Epsom street, I now looked at cases of street attacks and street rapes as well as home invasion attacks. I located one in Parnell in March 1992. Although it had taken place in the different environment of the street and in a car, the rape included all of Rewa's signature behaviours. This one was especially interesting to me not only for this but also for another reason. The victim was Rhonda McHardy, who has given permission for her full name to be used even though she has been given name suppression, as is the norm with victims of sexual assault. In this attack, Rhonda was struck on the head from behind as she reached her car parked on the side of the road. She feigned unconsciousness throughout the whole ordeal, which she said took some considerable time.

The importance of this information was that it showed that Rewa was acting out his perfect script. He did not have to alter anything in his recipe of sexual fantasies because of victim interference. This was him playing out his ritualistic fantasy exactly as he wanted.

We spoke with all our 'ladies' (we referred to our rape complainants as 'ladies', rather than 'victims' or 'women') who would be going to court. Rhonda, a very indomitable and intelligent woman, had reported to us in detail about what had taken place. She used the expression that 'she felt just like a prop for Rewa's performance' — this was straight out of a rape textbook from a behavioural science author. Rhonda knew that her attacker had raped before and that her life was in danger. Although a smart woman, she had no idea just how helpful her written statement and powerful delivery — both before court and during it — was in contributing to our growing understanding of Rewa, enabling us to unmask him and highlight his ritualistic behavioural patterns. As neatly said by criminal psychologist Nigel Latta in his book *Into the Darklands*: 'You do not find him in anything he says, you find him in what he does. What the guy says to you is, at face value, meaningless. What he did is where the real truth lies.'

The team also made inquiries all around the country — Rewa was a well-travelled man, especially as he enjoyed Malamute sledge racing and competed at a number of race meetings. We looked for reports of rapes or attacks at locations he had been at over the preceding years. A number of rape complaints emerged from these inquiries.

Two were of particular interest to me. The first was a rare stranger rape complaint, in Levin in August 1992; another street attack. It had enough behavioural consistencies to add to the list — plus Rewa had been in town that night. The other was a stranger intruder rape that occurred in Rotorua, the same city where the first DNA-linked rape of the original Operation Harvey series was committed. Rewa had lived with the Highway 61 motorcycle gang in Rotorua for a period. Again, his signature rape behaviours were present. In addition, we had a witness who had seen a person fitting Rewa's description, accompanied by what was described as a very large German shepherd dog, walking towards the victim's house at 3 a.m. The rape occurred shortly after 3 a.m. Rewa had been booked into a nearby motel that night as he was attending a Malamute race meeting. A large German shepherd is a good description of a Malamute at three o'clock in the morning.

Unfortunately, the victim in this case was inadequately dealt with by one particular police officer when she made her complaint.

As a result, despite our efforts to encourage her, she refused to join our ladies in court. I had, and still have, no doubt that Rewa committed this rape along with many others that did not quite meet the threshold for the Crown indictment.

Some male DNA that was not Rewa's was found on material at the scene of this rape. In one of our daily conferences at this time, Ruthers commented that this eliminated it from our series. I was sure of my analysis, and adamant that it had been a Rewa attack. I argued that the semen could easily be from someone else — maybe the victim's boyfriend or son. I had further inquiries made in Rotorua. Finally, the complainant volunteered information about a boyfriend, who was no longer in the country, being likely to be responsible for the DNA. But she continued to refuse to join the other ladies in court. I understood and respected her decision. She was not able to recover from the poor treatment she had received from the police officer initially involved.

Again, while obviously not Operation Harvey's fault, the poor treatment of a rape complainant by at least one staff member on the original investigation meant that this rape — one I was convinced that Rewa had committed — would be left off the indictment.

Two separate attacks on women in Mt Eden, in June 1993, were considered to be possible Rewa offences. In both cases the women had been going for a run early in the morning. However, because one woman lost consciousness while the other fought off the attack, there was no behavioural evidence to link the attacks to Rewa. Operation Running Man, which had been set up to catch this offender, was unsuccessful. We now put together a photographic montage of eight males, including Rewa, and one of the ladies identified him from it. Because the other offence was geographically and chronologically close, they were both included as prosecution cases. We were, however, relying on one identification made by one lady three years after the event. This meant this was evidentially the weakest of all the cases that were put before the court.

Many other rapes within the timeframe and in places frequented by Rewa were analysed, but either there was not enough behavioural evidence, or (in some cases) the victim had lost consciousness and there was no behavioural link at all. Without any other evidence, these also fell short of the evidential threshold for presentation in court.

THE LAST CASE to be included in the indictment was an attack in Ponsonby on 5 January 1995 — the one for which Rewa had a 'wanted to interview' alert. It occurred in a very short street that we knew Rewa had frequented a lot. This was typical offending in a geographical context, whereby he had little patches in suburbs that he regularly frequented and in which he committed his offences — not just intruder rapes but also lesser crimes. These were also places he was 'turned over' by police patrols as he wandered the streets or drove his vehicle, alone and in the early hours of the morning.

The victim in this case had woken to find a man on top of her, straddling her body. He struck her in the face several times; then, after a struggle, threw her onto her stomach and tied her hands behind her back. He then searched her purse — and left.

Having managed to remove the offender's balaclava during the struggle, the complainant gave the local police a detailed description and said she would be able to recognise him if she saw him again. A few days later, she identified Malcolm Rewa from photos of 65 men who fitted her description. This is noteworthy — the law requires a minimum of eight photographs in an identification montage. Eight was what had been used with the Running Man victims.

Even though this lady was positive about her identification, she asked to see Rewa in person so as to be absolutely sure. The 'Wanted to interview' alert was issued, but despite locating the address of Rewa's partner, in Māngere, and visiting it twice, police failed to locate him. Further inquiries also failed to find Rewa, so the case file was inactivated with a 'person of interest' entry being made into the national database in April 1995. As noted in the IPCA report into the handling of the Malcolm Rewa investigation, this is a common practice and not to be criticised, as the person is more likely to be located 'on the street' than in any particular location.

And it had the desired result. Rewa was detained at a routine traffic stop at the end of May that year. He was interviewed at Balmoral police station by one of the officers who had originally sought him in Māngere in January 1995. During this interview, Rewa denied any involvement in the Ponsonby attack, claiming to have not been in Auckland at the time. He also said he'd had a beard for almost a year; the victim in the Ponsonby attack had described him as clean-shaven (remember, also, that she'd already picked his photograph out of a montage of 65). The interviewing officer did not ask Rewa why he had spent several months ignoring the police's attempts to contact him.

Rewa now agreed to take part in an identification parade at Ponsonby police station, but this did not happen — police could not quickly find the required number of other men similar in appearance to Rewa. He was released on the understanding that the police would contact him when the parade had been arranged. Unsurprisingly, after a couple of weeks it became clear that he was no longer willing to cooperate.

During the following month, further inquiries revealed that Rewa had lied about his beard, but as he could not be located the investigation stalled. To complicate matters, in July, Rewa's lawyer made a complaint against police on Rewa's behalf, claiming that he was being harassed through the ongoing attempts to contact him. This of course had to be investigated, which took until November 1995 and concluded that there was no misconduct by the investigating officers.

The last activity on the Ponsonby case was in December 1995. It involved an unsuccessful attempt by a Ponsonby officer to clear up the alibi he was given by Rewa when he had first spoken to him months earlier. The case was then filed. This timing aligns directly with the commencement of the Operation Atlas offences.

When this file arrived on my desk for analysis, around May 1996, I was stunned — and incredulous that this attack had not been discovered in our search during Operation Atlas. Was it because it was recorded as an aggravated robbery, which would not have registered as significant in either the crime squad book or the ESR forms — if indeed, any entry ever existed in either of these? I was livid that the detectives, and police officers generally, who had attended and investigated this 'aggravated robbery' had not considered the importance of this event to Operation Atlas, given that it had occurred solidly within the Operation Atlas area and only ten months before that operation commenced. As part of Atlas there were public meetings in Ponsonby to get the public on board to watch out for and report any suspicious behaviour due to this very active intruder rapist. And yet no one who saw this file picked up on its possible — even likely — relevance.

Perhaps the answer lies in the sheer volume of serious crime and therefore the workload of the detectives who investigate these attacks. It is of course possible that the nature of my work gave me special insight into the significance of other attacks on women; but given that Operation Park was a pretty hot topic in Auckland at the time and we had even asked the public to watch out for peepers and peerers, it did not sit well with me that none of the officers involved had recognised the significance of the fact that an intruder wearing a balaclava (not mentioned in the IPCA report) had entered the home of a woman living alone, in the early hours of the morning. They hadn't twigged to the fact that him waking her by jumping on her in her bed was a sexually motivated attack. While technically it could have been an aggravated robbery or aggravated burglary, the motivation for the home invasion should have screamed out to those investigating. It certainly would have done so post-1995.

During Operation Park we had looked back through Joseph Thompson's criminal history. In the early 1990s, in the middle of his attacks, he had been disturbed in a house in Papatoetoe in the early hours. He had been standing at the foot of the bed of the woman who lived there alone. She awoke before he could establish any control and he left without the matter going any further — but was located in the vicinity by an on-the-spot uniformed patrol. Thompson quickly coughed to burglary and pleaded guilty — likely because he realised how close he had come to being picked up for an intruder sexual attack. A straight burglary conviction would not expose what his night-time activity had really been about.

It was the same with Rewa, who was eventually convicted for the Ponsonby attack on a charge of 'assault with intent to commit sexual violation' — not aggravated robbery or aggravated burglary. It is hard to imagine how the Ponsonby investigation did not identify Rewa as a sexually motivated intruder. In my opinion, this must have been embarrassing for the police and for the police hierarchy. Regardless of the IPCA's seemingly charitable view that it was not so recognised because in law it was an aggravated robbery, this was an intruder attack on a woman in her bed. It should have been recognised by someone involved as a sexual attack in the zone of Operation Atlas. If this had happened, we could have been six months ahead in our final identification of Rewa as our offender and some of his victims could have been spared their trauma.

It is also interesting that while the Ponsonby detective was, rightly, hunting for Rewa from early in 1995 through to November, when the harassment complaint was filed, we had no attacks in the central Auckland area for which we could place Rewa in the frame. Was that coincidence? I didn't think so. It was the same old story: put pressure on the street-smart offender, and he either stops or offends somewhere else. Remember Dan Dudson — Constable Harris had his number in East Auckland so Dan moved elsewhere to burgle. In mid-1995, Rewa offended for the only time we knew of over the Harbour Bridge, in Takapuna. The moment the heat was off, after the filing of the complaint, Rewa made up for lost time by committing the Atlas rapes right bang back in the central Auckland suburbs of Sandringham, One Tree Hill, Remuera, Mt Eden and Ponsonby — five rapes in two months. This also clearly showed how organised and controlled Rewa was in his rampage at this time.

I am not one to criticise the men and women in the trenches who make on-the-spot decisions based on where they are, their case-load at the time, and bosses who might have some other pressing duty for them. There are plenty sitting in a safe, air-conditioned office, in possession of all the facts, and the result, who are able to pass judgement. That's a little like looking at the answers to a cryptic crossword and considering how obvious they are from the questions provided. But there are some things that would have helped.

Rewa was released because, in the early hours of the morning, insufficient similar-looking men could be found for an identification parade. In retrospect, this was clearly a mistake. Rewa had been avoiding being questioned for months, so I would have thought he was not a prospect for release. However, I was not present and there may well have been other considerations of which I was unaware. But with all the changes in our laws, many of which assist the criminal, why did we not get the right to hold a suspect for twelve hours or longer while inquiries are being made? Many other countries appear to have such a helpful tool for this sort of situation. This would have allowed enough time for seven males fitting Rewa's description to be found and the identification parade carried out. The proof that he did not have a beard at the time of the attack could also have been established. Rewa would then most certainly have been arrested for that aggravated burglary/robbery; there may even have been consideration of a sexual charge. This would have meant that the file would still have been active as a prosecution file when Operation Atlas kicked off in November. Perhaps then, someone would have made the connection.

My penultimate comment about this file is the complaint of harassment made by Rewa's lawyer, which made the hunter become the hunted. This is an old trick. Lawyers send what is called a 'stinger' to accomplish exactly that goal: to take the heat off their client and take the detective out of the game. I have had a number of stingers during my career, and I recall a relieving boss in Papakura, an old-school detective inspector, dealing directly with one of these. He sent a rapid reply to the lawyer explaining that he would expect his detectives to hunt down suspects, because that was their job. Pity he wasn't working in Ponsonby in 1995. Many old detectives feel that, in the modern world, the balance between hunter and hunted has been forever lost in favour of the bad guys. If the file had still been with the CIB, rather than with professional standards, perhaps the result would have been different.

Finally, some checking would have revealed that Rewa had been convicted of burgling this very Ponsonby house back in the early 1980s. Meaning that this street was one of his targeted hit zones way back then, including this actual house.

WITH REWA ARRESTED and charged, the massive job of file preparation was now our focus. There was some new ground to cover, too. As expected, Rewa pleaded not guilty to the early holding charges, and we knew he would do the same for every charge we put in the final indictment. Unlike Joseph Thompson's case, where there was just two weeks between his guilty pleas and his sentencing, we had a bit more time up our sleeves; but there was still a lot of work to do.

We had not yet made a decision as to which attacks we would or could proceed with for the indictment, but our team members were all of one view. Every attack that reached the evidential threshold would be in front of the court on one indictment, rather than a select group of attacks being presented. Neither would we have them broken up with the DNA-linked charges on one indictment and the behavioural-based charges on another.

Rewa's designated counsel changed after the original one took up a position as a judge. The next one on the list was barrister Paul Dacre, a very capable ex-prosecutor with the Crown in Auckland.

But barrister Barry Hart had already been to visit Rewa in prison. According to Hart, Rewa wanted him to defend him. Again, an old trick, the upshot of which was that both Hart and Dacre represented Rewa, and the taxpayers paid double. Hart had won the first skirmish before we had even got into the ring. While we could do nothing about that, we made sure he won very little from then on.

All the files on my list were checked for exhibits that could be examined for forensic evidence tying them to Rewa. There were two for which there was a slim hope of a DNA link. I was very pleased that one of these was the street attack in Parnell where the victim — Rhonda McHardy — had feigned unconsciousness. This was because Rhonda's account underpinned Rewa's signature. It was also important because it brought into play attacks outside the victim's home. I was confident of the behaviour being clearly Rewa's signature, but because it was a street attack a jury might have difficulty linking it to the home-intruder rapes if we had to rely on the behavioural evidence alone. The other rape was significant because it was a particularly violent attack, on a woman in Māngere, who was chronologically and geographically near to Susan Burdett. This attack was also full of bloody rage and violence. The woman received such a severe beating to her face that her own family found her unrecognisable.

The DNA samples for these two cases were small and needed to be sent to the UK for special forensic analysis that could not be completed in New Zealand at that time. But the DNA result that came back linked both of these attacks to the Operation Harvey series.

This was compelling support for the criminal behavioural analysis that had linked the crimes in the first place. They were the only two 'behavioural' crimes with any forensic samples and now both were confirmed forensically as part of the series and the responsibility of one person: Malcolm Rewa, the Lone Wolf. This strengthened all the cases that relied on behavioural evidence, some of which were further supported by some other form of evidence, such as shoe impressions, Rewa having a connection to the area, or some other similar evidence.

The final count on the indictment from the 27 separate attacks included 1 murder, 32 rapes, 2 attempted rapes, 1 assault with intent to rape, 4 attempts to sexually violate, 3 aggravated woundings and 2 abductions, occurring from December 1987 through to May 1996. Most of these attacks occurred in central Auckland suburbs and South Auckland, but also included one in Rotorua, one in Levin and one in Takapuna. The case would not go to trial until a couple of years later.

10. PORA THE SPEED HUMP

CRIMINAL PROFILING HAD NOW HELPED us catch two serial rapists — a win for the police and the public. Operation Harvey had been a successful exercise in police investigative process, a tremendous team effort on a massive inquiry. As a team we were led brilliantly by Ruthers, and surmounted numerous new challenges never faced before; ground-breaking stuff. But there was one subject that always divided the team. It was the one speed hump that would always haunt the operation: Teina Pora.

This Māori teenager, later found to have brain deficiencies as a result of foetal alcohol spectrum disorder, was an early suspect after shooting his mouth off about a baseball bat he had seen down a drain in Manukau. He was soon cleared — after all, the baseball bat most likely to have been the murder weapon was lying next to Susan Burdett's body, and the semen found at the scene did not belong to Pora. However, in March 1993 Pora was charged by Ruthers and Mark Williams for the murder after he made a damning confession that he was present at the scene. He later retracted this confession, but he and his counsel could not seem to shrug it off over two trials, the first in 1994 and a retrial in 2000. Justice would come much later.

From the outset, I spoke out against Pora's involvement in the Burdett murder. It was Rewa's behaviour that made it clear to me that Pora had not been there with him at Susan Burdett's house. This decision of mine was totally behaviourally based — I knew from the profile and signature of Rewa's offending that he was a loner; he would not have had anyone with him for any criminal enterprise, let alone a planned rape. I was aware that Mitford and Lambo were also outspoken about Pora not being present, based on other factors to do with identifications, shortcomings regarding associations between Rewa and Pora, and the interview with Pora.

At this point the phrase 'criminal profiling' needs to be clarified due to all the media and hype surrounding it, especially on television and around Operations Park and Harvey. Criminal profiling is a process that arises after a behavioural analysis of a stranger crime such as rape has been completed. Once a full behavioural and geographic analysis of the scene, the complainant statement, exhibits, forensics, witness statements, precursor offending, victimology (links between victims) and any other relevant information (excluding perceived suspects) is completed, an effort is made to project a 'shadow' of the offender type from this analysis. While on TV they might come up with marital status, work type and other personal details, those aren't the sorts of information the police record! We're looking for something much more constructive and workable from the data actually available to us. We want to identify those characteristics of the offender that we can search to take us directly to that offender;

a system that would filter out suspects from tens of thousands of people in broad categories.

So, behavioural analysis comes first. Doing this allows us to understand our offender through his displayed behaviour at the scene. I learnt from John Douglas that if you want to understand Picasso, study his paintings; if you want to understand your offender, study his crime.

I did just that. Throughout Operations Atlas and Harvey I continued to read everything I could on rape behaviour. Not just the commercial books, but also those that went deeper into investigative processes to identify offenders from their behaviour: the nuts and bolts of drivers, motives, fantasy and behaviour. This complemented all the New Zealand rape files, both solved and unsolved, that I was also reading.

IN MY PERSONAL appraisal in June 1998, carried out by Mitford, I made it clear I believed that the conclusion of my expert analysis was this: there was only one offender present at the rape and murder of Susan Burdett — Malcolm Rewa.

At first glance, most would consider Rewa to be a well-socialised villain. He was involved in a gang, which many join because of a need to belong, to have a family, and form strong ties to others in the group. They refer to each other as brothers and the gang as their family. But in my experience these are very dysfunctional families, with violence and drug dealing the norm, and most newcomers being coerced by the biggest and most senior members in the gang to commit crimes.

Rewa was also a member of a touch rugby oldies team representing Auckland. Again, this might indicate that he was a team player rather than a loner. And he was involved in Malamute sledge racing — again, a social group. So, he was well known in a number of circles — or was he? Who from any of these groups really knew him, sat around chewing the fat with him, knew anything about him of a personal nature? No one.

By behavioural definition, Rewa was, as many intruder serial sexual offenders are, really a loner. I later profiled another lone serial rapist, and he was a well-established member of a criminal motorcycle gang. Perhaps surprisingly, the best place for a loner to hide is surrounded by people — by 'getting lost in a crowd'. This was part of Rewa's plan of survival. He learnt early that he could never trust anyone. Being part of a group or gang was, therefore, just a means to an end for him. In the gang he was the 'master at arms', a gang's equivalent to the political party whip. This meant he kept others in their place using violence, while also planning any violent activity against anyone threatening the gang. It was a position of brutal domination; a place where he was automatically feared. He did not get his nickname, 'Hammer', from a carpentry apprenticeship.

After earlier experiences of being brought down legally by associating with others in criminal activities, from the early 1980s onwards Rewa offended on his own. He had learnt that when he offended alone, there was no one to snitch on him, no concerns about undercover police, no one to let him down in a crisis, and no communication with others that could be recorded. When 'turned over' by police while prowling the streets in his truck, which had 'Lone Wolf' printed on the front, he was always alone. He even referred to himself as the Lone Wolf. I can't recall exactly when I started calling the offender I was profiling the 'Lone Wolf'; it could well have just been coincidence.

He burgled alone and he raped alone, hiding behind a mask of anonymity. He allowed no one to enter, or be part of, his sexual fantasies, his very private world. Like so many others with twisted personal sexual fantasies and fixations, no one else was welcome in that place. Even his victims were props for his orchestrated fantasy. They were blindfolded not only to prevent identification, but also to prevent them viewing his behaviour. In all the rapes for which Rewa was convicted, no one else was ever seen to be present.

Was such a man likely to take a seventeen-year-old, 'dull-witted' blabbermouth gang prospect, from an opposing gang, on a night out where he planned to commit a rape? Would he have taken this boy — indeed, anyone — to view his sexual inadequacies and be party to his personal fantasies? No. Rewa lived by intimidation and violence, and survived by living alone in a world that no one else could share or enter.

My views never changed; I continued to focus solely on the behavioural argument that Rewa would not have taken anyone with him to a rape scene. I never viewed Pora's interview, nor had anything to do with the identification and the alleged connections between Rewa and Pora. In fact, I had nothing to do with Pora at all; to this day, I have never met him. Despite that, I would later play a role in the final chapter of the Pora saga.

There was one other factor that didn't make sense if Pora *had* been at the scene with Rewa. To support his story and explain the semen found at the Burdett scene that did not belong to him, Pora had dobbed in two of the most senior Mongrel Mob members in Māngere. After their blood was collected and they were eliminated, Pora tried to add some others from the Mongrel Mob; they were also eliminated. These were powerful figures in the area where Pora was living — and very dangerous people to dob in for any crime, let alone a murder. Particularly when they were not even there. It also brought heat down on the gang that Pora associated with.

Why not dob in Rewa? For many of us the answer was simple — because Pora didn't even know him. If he had, he would have dobbed him in.

WHILE THE INITIAL thrust of the prosecution was that the conviction of Pora was not a consideration when it came to Rewa, this course altered closer to Rewa's trial, when it was clear we could not ignore him. Inquiries were being made by some members of the team aimed at demonstrating an association between Rewa and Pora. I was not involved in these inquiries, nor in how they were obtained or presented at the subsequent court case. And why would I be? All the team knew my views regarding Pora's involvement in Susan Burdett's murder and rape — there was none.

Karl Wright-St Clair, who was O/C Suspects, was also against the idea of Pora being involved. His view had been formed during the earlier investigation of Pora, in which he had participated. Years earlier he had thought that Pora was just a mouthy young fool who had talked his way into the murder scene. Karl was a little quieter, but then he had a career to consider while us older South Auckland detectives — Mitford, Lambo, and myself — had no intention of climbing further up the ladder to glory.

But a homicide inquiry is not a democratic process. Ruthers was the boss, and he was strongly supported by Detective Sergeant Mark Williams, who managed the file regarding Pora's involvement. They directed the Crown, and that is where it stayed. Prison was where Pora stayed. It was not vindictive; they sincerely believed that Pora was present at Burdett's murder.

This division of opinion within the police lingered long after Rewa's trial and came to a head many years later, as I knew it would. It was a pity, because apart from this, the team was tight and the operation was highly successful and well run. But they would not let Pora go — one mistake, but a monster of a mistake that had an impact on everything that happened afterwards.

ON THE FIRST morning of his trial, Malcolm Rewa pleaded guilty to all the DNA-link rapes apart from the Susan Burdett rape and murder. That was seven rape convictions straight after the bell.

It was a surprise, but not one that worried us; to the contrary, in fact, because he had now admitted to all the behaviours in those rapes that were replicated in the others that he continued to plead not guilty to. My behavioural evidence was now very much in focus.

Our ladies each gave their evidence, even those who already had guilty pleas for the attacks on them — they did so in order to support the other ladies, even though they had not yet met each other. The ladies were all compelling, in different ways. They spoke of their experiences being attacked in their own home — gagged, blindfolded, bound and raped — how they had feared for their lives. The varying emotions — trauma, embarrassment, anger — evident in the strange, seemingly unfair environment of a court is a massive hurdle to get over. We expect so much from victims, and all we can do is try to get each one through it the best they can. Each victim is a different person handling each problem that lands on their plate in a different way. We were very fortunate in the level of cooperation we received from our ladies on Operation Harvey.

Of course, the ultimate hurdle for any victim is to learn to live with the trauma they've experienced and to get through the rest of their lives. They will all take different routes to do this. I am sure that their experiences with Rewa still lie heavy with all our ladies, especially on certain dates and when similar incidents emerge in the media. Many of them summed up their court appearance in Jan Jordan's 2008 book *Serial Survivors*, for which I helped arrange interviews. Although it's a tough, emotional read, it's also a revealing one.

The ladies took us close to home base with puissant, persuasive and coherent evidence from the witness box. Some even spat responses back at barrister Barry Hart, who seemed to do most of their cross-examinations. As the trial continued, most of the ladies grew to hate Hart as much as Rewa. They wanted to take back control from Rewa and Hart by having the court and the witness box as their castle, their safe haven. They did this in various personal and unusual ways. Some did it by having a close family friend with them: others achieved it with personal touches of perfume, glitter or favourite personal items. They were totally successful — partly due to their compelling evidence from the witness box and, I hope, partly due to the preparation given to them by our victim support officers, Veronica and Cath, as well as the rest of the team, both police and the Crown. All we now needed was the behavioural evidence to back up their efforts.

One of our 27 ladies had been sexually attacked by Rewa way back in the '70s when she was a nurse in a nursing home near where Rewa was waiting for his first wife to have a baby. He must have become bored with waiting around and gone out for a stalk. Giving evidence was a massive effort for this lady, as she had to dig into her buried past and bring everything back again twenty years later. I think she did this for all the other ladies involved and for Susan Burdett. A brave effort — she could have refused, and we all would have understood. Of course, some of Rewa's behavioural signature was already imbedded even back then and displayed during the attack — it was further support for our behavioural evidence.

This was the first trial at which I gave evidence as an expert witness. As I had for Joseph Thompson, I had prepared a chart summarising the Crown case and highlighting all the behavioural characteristics of the attacks Malcolm Rewa had been charged with. It had a long line of columns covering every aspect of the crimes — dates, locations, events that occurred, behaviours that were present or not present, etc. Each attack was on a separate row and had the columns filled in as appropriate for that particular crime. Colour coding helped to make sense of the wealth of information. Sitting in that court through the days, weeks and months of the ladies' evidence, I updated the chart in the odd case where some of the facts noted on there were not confirmed in the witness's evidence on the stand, or, in some cases, where their evidence went further due to the powerful advocacy of the Crown team: Auckland Crown prosecutor Simon Moore and Paul Davison QC, supported by Gina McGrath.

I believe that we all learnt from this trial — both the ladies and the police team, which included the Crown. Some of the ladies, I suspect, initially viewed the police as being hard-nosed, intransigent, mulish and single-minded — all carved from the same rockface, so to speak. They were surprised when Ruthers made them a coffee or a cup of tea, or they laughed over nothing in particular with Lambo. One lady wore her favourite rose into the witness box, and was surprised to discover that I could immediately identify it as French Lace. Obviously she had not imagined that a hard-nosed detective sergeant would have an interest in roses when, in fact, I had over 200 growing at home in a garden that had become part of the local garden ramble scene. French Lace was one of these roses.

In Jan Jordan's book *Serial Survivors*, she includes comments from these ladies specifically about us and the trial:

> 'They were all very caring and respectful. They all got on with their job, as far as I was concerned, very well. He was convicted and they won, the goodies won and the baddies lost. It was probably reassuring more than anything to see people like that in action.'

> 'You weren't just witnesses, you were actually a person to them, which was nice . . . I can't fault them.'

> 'As for the Police, the Harvey team, I felt that they became like a caring little family. I think they tried to make it as easy as they could for the victim — they looked after you. At a time like that, what more could you say, what more could you do?'

In turn I, at least, learnt a lot from our ladies. They knew a great deal more about rape behaviour than you would expect from random members of the public. You could argue that this came down to having lived through the experience, but I think it went deeper than that. Had they studied it after their experiences? Or is there a deep, inherent fear of being raped that's common to all women, due to the risks of encountering sexual predators? No girl or woman should have to live with the fear of potential violation.

HAVING ESTABLISHED MY expert status as a behavioural analyst by opening with my experience with Operation Park and what we'd learnt from that process, I used the updated chart — now totally accurate in terms of the ladies' evidence — to guide the jury through the behavioural aspects of the rapes. I took the court and the jury through each column in my chart, outlining the significance, and the commonality or rarity, of each particular behaviour. This evidence also demonstrated that the combination of features in this chart did not exist in any other of the hundreds of case files I had examined throughout my work as a detective. In the years since the trial, I never saw the co-existence of these particular features through all my reviews of rape cases, then closer to 1000 in number.

Paul Davison QC led my evidence-giving. We thought it went much better than expected, but the jury would be the judge of that. If they didn't agree with my evidence, a large number of the charges would fail — and therefore we would have failed the ladies who had stepped up so bravely and performed so well. It was a trying time for all concerned.

The courtroom was set up in an unusual way because of security concerns with regard to Rewa. It meant that Rewa was sitting partly behind and to the side of me. It was different when the ladies gave their evidence; there was no way he would have been permitted near them. I remember the big chart acting as a screen between them and Rewa when they first walked in, so they did not have to see him staring at them (the jury had their own, smaller, version). As I gave my evidence, Rewa taunted me throughout, but quietly so that Justice Noel Anderson could not hear him. Most of his remarks were obscene, and most involved wanting me to bend over so he could sexually violate me from the rear. It had the opposite effect to what Rewa intended, because I knew it meant my evidence was getting under his skin.

The clerk of the court did hear Rewa and asked me, during a break, if I wanted her to tell Justice Anderson about the taunts. I replied that this would only constitute a minor victory for Rewa and I wouldn't let him have that privilege. The witness box had been won by the ladies and he wouldn't be seizing back any control from me.

I had prepared myself for any attacks that Mitford, Davison and I thought might come my way from the defence during my cross-examination. But to be honest, I had expected more challenge than I got. Hart called my evidence 'Henwood's theory' to try to undermine it, but there was nothing more than that. It seemed a little lame in the end. Most of the predicted questions on which we had done our homework never got asked. Perhaps the more subtle Paul Dacre should have cross-examined me rather than the confrontational Barry Hart, who had built his reputation on fiery attacks, particularly on police. In my view, this was simply not a trial for that style of cross-examination.

Rewa then gave evidence, denying the rapes. To explain his semen being present at the Susan Burdett homicide scene, he claimed (in general terms) that he had had consensual sex with her at Māngere Mountain after sharing an ecstasy tablet in the afternoon before she was murdered. It was a ridiculous story that could not be believed by anyone who was not high on drugs. It was totally put to the sword by ESR's evidence provided by Dr SallyAnn Harbison, which was referred to as SallyAnn's 'semen migration assessment'. This assessment was based on the unlikely event that semen from unprotected sex would remain within Susan from the afternoon and then all night with Susan playing a competition evening of ten-pin bowling. Another factor refuting this explanation of Rewa's was, of course, that it meant someone *else* had broken into Susan's home after she'd returned from bowling, and attacked her and murdered her, leaving her naked from the waist down, her upper body covered and her legs off the bed — all three of which were behaviours that aligned with Rewa's modus operandi as shown in the DNA-linked rapes to which he had already pleaded guilty. And, of course, you would have to question why only Rewa's semen had been found. A coincidence too great to digest, I would have thought.

Rewa also claimed, again in general terms, that he was a woman magnet and didn't need to rape women. This claim was greeted with groans and derisive laughter from the ladies, many of whom were present when he gave his evidence. Of course it didn't fit with the fact that he'd already pleaded guilty to the DNA-linked rapes.

THE JURY TOOK some time to consider, as you would expect with so many charges on the indictment. After a three-month trial, a quick verdict would have given the defence grounds for an appeal. When they did return, at midnight on 29 May 1998, it was with convictions on almost all counts. Most of our team was present.

Three cases did not receive a verdict of guilty. The first two were the Running Man attacks in Mt Eden in June 1993, which relied solely on an identification made three years after the event. This was no surprise, as Justice Anderson had made enough comment regarding the danger of the identification. You could not help but feel sorry for these two ladies, who had given their best, but legally it just didn't reach the necessary standard for the jury to convict.

The other case was the Susan Burdett rape and murder; the jury could not agree on a verdict. This was a blow, and I knew immediately why the jury had had problems with it — Teina Pora was in the way, and his involvement made no more sense to the jury than it did to many of us. He didn't fit into the package we put before them. It spelt trouble for Mark and Ruthers, who would eventually have to deal with Susan Burdett's murder and rape again at a retrial. I hoped they would now reconsider Pora's involvement, but they didn't. They still firmly believed that Pora had been there.

On the positive side, all the other cases based on the behavioural evidence, some with other supporting evidence, received guilty verdicts. This was a massive result, at a massive serial rape trial. Nothing like it has been seen or heard before or since. It was a relief for me and a positive step towards the formation of a national rape/profiling squad.

Sitting in court when Rewa was sentenced to preventive detention, with 22 years before he could apply for parole, was one of my most satisfying court memories. Many of the ladies were present, as well as the women from the jury in the front row. In sentencing, Justice Noel Anderson was very direct in taking away any remaining power Rewa might have had, while focusing on the 'courage and dignity' of the ladies.

His final words will echo in the minds of those present to this day:

> Rewa, those are the wounds you have inflicted on these sisters
> of the legion of the brave and now you are going to pay for it.
> Stand up!

If some of the many ladies present found themselves shedding a tear at that moment, they were not alone. Even thinking about it now almost brings tears to my eyes — especially Justice Anderson's comments. I was hugely relieved at the outcome. It was certainly not Rewa's day centre-stage at the Auckland High Court.

The Lone Wolf was sent down — but the rape and murder of Susan Burdett was not finished with yet by a long way. Rewa was on trial again in December 1998 for this crime. He was convicted of the rape of Susan Burdett, but there was another hung jury regarding the murder charge. Pora was still in the way. I played no part in this second trial; this may have been because I was on the wrong side of the Pora argument and the chances were that my view would come out if I gave evidence before Pora's second trial which had been set down for 2000.

Another rape conviction for Rewa and 14 years of imprisonment concurrent with his present sentence — not much difference in real terms, as far as time in prison was concerned, but perhaps a good indicator of how a murder trial might go should Pora ever be eliminated from the equation. A murder conviction for Rewa would surely ensure that this savage Lone Wolf would never stalk the streets again.

But we did not have this yet, and it seemed as if we never would.

In effect, there was no real justice for Susan Burdett. Rewa received no additional sentence in real terms than he already had. No murder conviction at all for a murder many of us knew he had committed while another man — Teina Pora — was languishing in prison despite not being present when it took place.

11. BUILDING A TEAM TO CLIMB INSIDE THE MINDS OF MONSTERS

AFTER OPERATION HARVEY I BECAME briefly enmeshed in yet another homicide. Mitford and I were also in the driver's seat setting up what would become known as the Criminal Profiling Unit. Lambo was in the wings as the third man should we succeed in getting the new unit off the ground. We three had gained valuable profiling experience through Operation Park and Operation Harvey. Our goal was to establish a behavioural rape squad fit for the twenty-first century.

In a way, though, calling it the Criminal Profiling Unit was probably partly responsible for some misunderstanding of the unit we developed. While criminal profiling and building priority suspect lists was an important part of the unit's workload it was just one aspect of our work, with more emphasis probably on rape behaviour and the linking of offences to offences and offences to offenders. This is probably the reason why the unit is now known as the National Behavioural Unit. The media, however, were more interested in the criminal profiling element because that was seen as more 'sexy' and all over the TV.

To my knowledge, there was little if any of this 'linking' work in this field in New Zealand up until Operation Park kicked off, and it only came about in Park through desperation. An example of necessity being the mother of invention. Even though at that stage the behavioural linkage process was in its infancy, it was amazingly accurate and that was a pointer and a confidence builder for not only Operation Harvey but also the eventual creation of the CPU.

Establishing a new unit meant taking staff from the already thin blue line. We would need some younger staff, and at least one of our new team members had to be a woman. We were looking for someone with a degree in psychology first and foremost, along with direct police experience in the field. Initially we wouldn't need a theorist academic — perhaps later once the squad was developed and had more staff. To achieve all this we needed a good plan, a solid argument and powerful backing, especially as we were setting up in Auckland rather than Wellington.

One of the most resounding arguments was that we could not, morally, ever again allow another Thompson or Rewa to brutalise and poison women and girls for so many years. In her 1996 book *Caught by his Past*, journalist Jan Corbett made the compelling point that we had drug squads, burglary and car-theft squads, and fraud squads — but no rape squad. I spoke at numerous service club gatherings outlining the successes of Operations Park and Harvey to emphasise the fact that we needed to have a specialised squad to prevent this happening again. Four or five CIB non-commissioned officers, many of whom (including Simpo) had worked on these operations, headed off to the international criminal tribunal in The Hague to investigate the crimes committed during the Bosnian War, which had ended in December 1995 (although conflict continued in the region for some time). As hard as it was for the police to lose this number of experienced investigators, many of whom never returned, we were also now asking for three more very experienced frontline investigators for our new unit. South Auckland in particular suffered a mass loss from their number of experienced CIB staff over a very short period of time.

Thankfully we did get some powerful advocates on board, and on the back of the successes of Operations Park and Harvey, the Auckland Regional Commander, Brion Duncan, supported the setting-up of the unit. The department was politically, publicly and morally forced to give us the necessary approval along with a small budget, and we set up in a small room we described as our 'cupboard' in Harlech House in Ōtāhuhu, around November 1998. We took as many solved and unsolved rape files as we could find, along with rape investigation research books from around the world. That was about all we could fit into our confined space, along with some computers and stationery and some books of our own that we carried over as surplus from Operations Park and Harvey. I continued to read the rape files, complainant statements, and as much as I could absorb from a police library full of books on behavioural and psychological aspects of rape. We also purchased a number of new rape investigation books available internationally, either personally or using our small profiling unit budget.

INITIALLY, NEAR THE end of 1998, it was just Mitford and myself; Lambo joined us early in 1999. The aim was a squad of four, with the fourth member joining us some time in the future. We all doubted whether this would actually happen, as we'd been around long enough to know that the tight police budget meant this was pie in the sky. We had to prove our worth at this sorely needed work to have any chance of this becoming a realistic prospect. Although in the beginning we were financially supported by the four Auckland districts of Counties Manukau, Auckland Central, Waitematā and North Shore, we knew we were actually working for the whole country and at some stage would have to be financially supported accordingly. This came to pass a few years later when we became the National Criminal Profiling Unit. Being financed from Wellington HQ was not only much more sensible given our scope and remit, but also gave the unit a more long-term prospect.

One morning in early 2000, Mitford called Lambo and me into his office; although we had spread out a little and had a bit more space, this was still a squeeze. He announced that he had volunteered to join other New Zealand police at The Hague on war crimes duty with the United Nations criminal tribunal. He departed very shortly afterwards, leaving just the two of us remaining in the unit — again. I was now O/C, if one can be an O/C of a squad comprising only one staff member, which meant having to deal with all the administrative rubbish — normally done by a detective senior sergeant — but without any extra remuneration. There were promises of staff replacements, but Lambo and I were sceptical about anything happening anytime soon. The department's accountants now had the salary of the departed Mitford to balance the books somewhere else, and were not in a hurry to give anything back to us.

Mary Goddard, known to us all as Mog, migrated from the UK in 2004 and joined the unit a few months later. She held degrees in psychology and criminology and had specialised in rape behaviour analysis. She'd been working with the Serious Crime Analysis Section (SCAS), which was part of the National Crime and Operations Faculty in Bramshill, now the UK National Crime Agency and overseen by the Home Office. SCAS used an international behavioural database called ViCLAS, or the Violent Crime Linkage Analysis System. More than this, Mog was a perfect fit for our unit as she had worked in the field with drug abuse offenders — she wasn't just a theorist. We couldn't afford to lose her, despite having no approval for the budget and her role, so we placed her 'in the wings' at Harlech House, in a position below her qualification level, while we waited for all that to work through the system. Finally she became the new third member of our little unit in April 2005.

The staffing issue was always frustrating. The unit had been set up to have four staff with a detective senior sergeant as O/C. We had to wait six to eight months to even replace the third member, let alone the senior sergeant. It seemed clear to us that the powers that be had removed the third position to save money and we had to fight to get it back. Given this, what chance would we ever have of getting our fourth member?

However, things did begin to fall into place. Mog and I were the behavioural analysts while Lambo worked on the criminal profiling computer program, known as Zwaagsi, with the assistance of a part-time Frank van der Zwaag — our brilliant IT colleague from Operations Park and Harvey. It meant we were three plus one very important member who was invisible to the department and costing them next to nothing. Frank worked with Lambo into the early hours of many mornings for little reward except the knowledge that the computer system named in his honour was taking form.

BY 1999 OUR new unit had become operationally involved in stranger rapes and homicides around the country and a year later I began being involved in evidential briefs as an expert witness. We also delivered lectures and training at detective qualifying courses and induction courses, and at CIB training days. We were keen to get out among staff who we believed we could help. We wanted to ensure that they knew us, and knew we could offer valuable practical expertise for serious stranger crimes, particularly rape. At the same time, we were trying to engage the cynics, those who probably saw us as some office dwellers new off the block, working on the latest unhelpful Middle Earth ideas. Fortunately, Lambo and I were well known around the trenches and cases quickly started to roll in to add to the historical ones.

In 1995, before Operations Park and Harvey, there had been over 120 unsolved rapes in the Auckland metropolitan area that we knew about. Even after those two operations had cleared up 60 per cent of them, there were still a good number to work on. We had put aside the historical rape files that were neither Thompson's nor Rewa's so that they'd be available when we needed them. This was that time. From 1998 onwards, with the expert assistance of ESR and our behavioural analysis team, we solved many of those outstanding cases, including a few of the smaller rape series. None approached the scale of Park or Harvey, though some of the historical cases dovetailed with the active rape inquiries that were being brought to us.

Sue V and her team at ESR were now developing a DNA-testing technique — PCR or polymerase chain reaction — that exceeded the standard possible in the early 1990s. Very small samples taken at a scene could now result in either a match on the DNA database or, at the very least, a DNA result we could work with to identify the offender. In the early to mid-1990s, Sue reckoned they needed a sample the size of a 50-cent piece; now it was a fraction of that. While the process has improved massively since then, this was a great step forward for us given the exhibits available in historical rape files. Using this scientific advance, we achieved great success in solving many rape cases that fell within the Historic Cases Project. John Manning, who had by now retired as a sworn officer, was also involved, with considerable success. He returned in the role of ESR liaison, working from an office next to the profiling unit, and continued in that role for several years.

Another development was the Criminal Investigations (Bodily Samples) Act 1995, which had become law following Operation Park. The Act allowed bodily samples to be taken for use in criminal investigations — previously it had been voluntary, and if they refused you could try for a warrant but they'd have to be a pretty good suspect for you to get one. Now, the Act requires them to comply. It also authorised the establishment of a databank derived from the analysis of those samples, to be used in criminal investigations. The police now had national specialist teams whose task it was to obtain samples from all people with relevant criminal histories and to add these to the rape database. As the DNA databank grew, we scrambled around for exhibits (samples of bodily tissue) that still existed in historical rape cases. Whenever we found an exhibit with potential DNA, it was sent to Sue. Some exhibits were fifteen years old or more, but just because they were old cases it didn't mean that solving them wasn't important. These historical rapes had victims who still needed a result from us. After all, we had failed them for fifteen years already — longer in some cases.

I recall one woman whose rape we solved through this system writing to me afterwards to thank us. 'I can now walk down the street knowing that none of the men I see was the one who raped me that night.' Another rape victim said, 'I am free to walk to the dairy for the first time in twelve years.' *This* was why resolving historical rapes was so important and so satisfying.

A further aspect of the DNA databank was the Familial DNA Project, for which Sue V asked me to be the contact police sponsor. The concept was that while the offender for a crime might not have DNA in our databank, a close relative such as a brother or father — who would have very similar DNA — might, and this could lead us directly to the offender. The guru in this area, Jonathan Whittaker, had achieved successful familial screening results in the UK, and he came over to New Zealand to discuss and lecture on the project. We discussed advantages and possible issues relating to the New Zealand environment. The project went forward. It achieved immediate success in a high-profile unsolved homicide case in Auckland. Although the offender did not have a sample in the DNA databank, his brother did. Another success notched up by Sue Vintiner and her colleagues.

Forensic science was taking great leaps forward in solving crimes. Those involved in the fight to solve stranger crime were increasingly those who wore white coats in a laboratory — but they could not do their work without the detectives doing the groundwork to acquire the exhibit samples and get cases to court.

Alongside the DNA databank, Lambo was working with Frank on improving the Zwaagsi database so that it was comprehensive, up to date and viable. This would provide us with the engine to generate and distribute an accurate suspect list for inquiries. The lists we'd used in Park and Harvey had been successful, but we knew we could achieve greater success with much shorter lists in which the suspect would place nearer the top. This was particularly important for single rapes — these would not have a team of twenty detectives tasked solely with the job of blooding large numbers of suspects the way Operations Harvey and Park had had, so we had to be more accurate and targeted in generating priority suspect lists. As far as I am aware, Zwaagsi was very much a unique New Zealand development, based on data held on the Wanganui Computer and made possible by having one police department covering the whole country.

Zwaagsi provided one set of data for generating priority suspect lists, based on information from charge sheets. The other set needed was, of course, the behavioural database. We started by trying to create one ourselves. Although it was useful — and an improvement on me having all the offenders' various behaviours stashed in my head — it was not ideal.

The identification and accurate classification of human behaviour is not a simple task. A trained human brain can identify and analyse subtle nuances of behaviour, in a way that a regular computer cannot. But some, more complicated, systems do a very good job of it. We studied many computerised behaviour systems that already existed and chose ViCLAS to replace our naive attempt. Built in Canada by a large team of investigators, psychiatrists and IT experts specifically for the police, the Violent Crime Linkage Analysis System is purpose-built for carrying out case linkage and behavioural analysis of stranger sexual offences. ViCLAS can store, collate and link data of offences falling into a defined set of criteria, including stranger sexual offending. Its cornerstone is a standardised methodology for data collection and entry, meaning that cases can be compared internationally, providing a very large database for comparison.

Our new British recruit Mog had worked successfully with

ViCLAS in the UK, and confirmed that this was the behavioural database we needed. Following support from a number of quarters, including my cadet mate Ted Cox, who was now the detective superintendent in charge of Auckland Metro, we managed to get the go-ahead. This was to be Mog's baby, naturally, as she was already on board with the concept. She was soon on a plane to Canada to be trained and obtain the New Zealand Police licence for the program.

Now, 'all' we needed to do was load all our known offenders and outstanding cases onto the behavioural database! Mog was a very busy woman from that moment on. Although she received assistance from time to time, she had to monitor all input data to ensure the credibility of the system.

VERY EARLY IN our time at the Criminal Profiling Unit — even before Mitford had left—we realised that one of the most important aspects of analysing any rape file was the victim interview. Many of the victim statements we were reading were handwritten or typed, not video-recorded, and ranged from very good to inadequate. Across the board, the art of interviewing seemed to have become forgotten as a fundamental core duty, when in reality it is central to almost all police investigations — it often forms the nucleus of an inquiry. There were a number of reasons for this. One was video interviews being avoided by most suspects; another was the lack of available time for frontline staff to conduct a proper interview. I also think there was a lack of emphasis in general on the importance of talking and listening to people.

Badly taken statements are not just of little value — they can also take an inquiry in the wrong direction, as had happened in homicides I reviewed. One such case I worked on involved immigrants to New Zealand of whom few, if any, could speak English. The interviews did contain basic information, obtained from a question-and-answer-style interview through an interpreter, but what was missing was the very essence of what a good statement should contain. There was no indication of the character or psyche of the interviewees, and the big picture of what the interviewees were trying to put across was missing. We knew little about them or what they were trying to say. Instead, we got a stick figure built from staccato bits of information clearly obtained through leading questions, as it was mixed with police jargon. There was no soul to the statement. Trying to analyse or glean information from such statements was like biting down on a dry piece of toast. Some statements may well have looked very nice, but criminal investigations are not a beauty contest. It is the interviewees' actual words and the way they are replicated that forms the heart of their statement. Ensuring accuracy and detail are at the core of any skilful interview.

In fairness, I cannot recall having much, if any, police college training on obtaining statements. This skill was learnt on the hoof from experienced police officers and detectives once we were on the street. These older detectives knew the art of conversation. We did some reading, which revealed a few basic concepts. Put the interviewee at ease. Ask them to take their time and, in their own words and in as much detail as they can, tell us from the beginning what happened. Anything that needs to be expanded on should be obtained with open-ended questions and without any leading questions.

In 2001, I sent a report directly to the director of investigations at Police National HQ — the most senior CIB officer in the country. This report focused on the importance of sourcing accurate and detailed information from victims of sexual offences. It stated that the interviewing of suspects, witnesses and complainants had been neglected, and this had caused the police serious problems in many investigations. In the report I also recommended giving serious consideration to recording interviews with rape victims and important witnesses in homicides on DVD, to demonstrate the accuracy of the interview and that information was not obtained through leading questions. This would also result in more detailed interviews, as the interviewer would be able to listen for gaps or areas to be expanded on instead of trying to keep writing or typing the statement as it was being spoken.

Video-recorded interviews have another advantage. In controversial investigations, especially homicides and rapes, witnesses often wish to recant on their statements. There are numerous reasons for this, including changing allegiances. If a witness or complainant wishes to change his/her story — and this happened in a highly controversial police shooting — it's much easier to escape or avoid a statement made when it has been written down by someone else. The witness or complainant can simply say that they didn't say what was recorded, or that the interviewer had made an assumption about what the interviewee had meant and had written down their own understanding of the interviewee's words.

There is some truth, however, in the suggestion that police officers write down what they interpret from what they hear, or what they assume someone means. This was proved to us when we studied statements made by rape complainants. The language used was often police parlance or, worse, police jargon — not at all what the interviewee would have said. Accordingly, it was not an accurate record of the interview. By jargon I'm referring to technical terminology such as 'custody', 'watchhouse', 'victimology'. An example of police parlance is: 'I exited the car and proceeded to the rear of the house.'

We also believed that somewhere down the track the DVD-recorded interview of a rape complainant could be played to the court — the victim would not then have to repeat the traumatic details, chapter and verse, to a jury (although she would, of course, still be required to be cross-examined). This was another reason why interviews needed to be recorded accurately.

I never heard anything back. I made an official information request in 2019 for a copy of the report, but was advised by the police that it could not be located. However, a subsequent report, dated in 2004, which referred to a copy of the original report being attached, *was* released under an official information request.

Three years after I sent my report, while I was lecturing at a detective's course at the Police College, I spoke with the training manager of the college — who agreed that interviewing was critical in any police investigation and was not given the time and training it deserved. I mentioned to him that I had submitted a report on this some years earlier that appeared to me to have been ignored, and suggested he follow it up at his level. To his credit, he did follow it up and finally it became an important issue nationally. I was amazed that someone in the right place could remove the cobwebs from a report that had been sitting idle for years. In 2005, a national project called the Interviewing Project began. Better late than never, I supposed.

By this time, Lambo had taken up the interviewing issue within our office and had carried out considerable study on the subject. In addition to disseminating his practical knowledge, he was also lecturing at the Police College to detectives and on detective induction courses, and had done so for years. When the Interviewing Project kicked off in 2005, naturally we assumed that our office, and Lambo, would take a lead role, given that we had been the instigators or, at the very least, a catalyst for its inception. We had also already done much research and lecturing on the topic. But no. Instead of taking advantage of the existing expertise and resources, the project was taken over by Police National Headquarters. A non-sworn person was contracted to start from scratch. We were scheduled to meet this person in June that year at the profiling office at Harlech House.

This non-sworn contractor, who came to be known in our office as 'Gollum', arrived bristling with hostility. Naturally, the meeting did not go well. It was clear that she did not want our involvement. I figured this was because she wanted the project to be her baby and needed us out of the equation. After a robust and hostile exchange that lasted for over an hour, she left. On leaving our office, she requested to see what an interview room looked like. Thus are silos built and valuable resources squandered to reinvent the wheel. Mog, Lambo and I immediately documented what had just taken place; we knew it would become a hot topic very soon. (Interestingly, this report by Gollum was one of only two documents released by police from my many official information requests.)

Once Middle Earth had set the ball in motion, we became side-lined. I had to console a very irate Lambo, telling him to forget it. At least the issue of interviewing was now getting traction, even if we had been left out of things. Did it really matter who brought the baby into this world, as long as it happened? We put it aside but continued to lecture at detective courses, using the same lecture notes on interviewing techniques as we had done for years.

The final project document produced by Gollum a year or so later was to my eye more or less what Lambo had been lecturing on for years — only with a budget and a training regimen attached. I sent Lambo down to a meeting at Police College, but the superintendent running the meeting was confronted by Gollum who objected to Lambo's presence. Lambo was ordered to leave the meeting before it had even started. In my opinion his treatment was a disgrace. I felt very sorry for him. He did not receive the credit I thought he deserved for his massive input into the topic over the years. My initial report was never mentioned again. There have, however, been some improvements in interviewing techniques.

MY STUDY OF rape statements and international rape investigation methodology, as well as my experiences providing expert evidence in courts around the country, deepened my interest in understanding more about rape behaviour. My view was that there is no point in having this knowledge and expertise unless it is put to a practical use. This meant taking what we knew to those in the trenches, court rooms and training rooms around New Zealand. We seized every opportunity to do this. This work took me to courts from Invercargill to Auckland, to murder and rape scenes and inquiries all over the country. These were usually the most notorious, well-reported rape cases — stranger offender, or potentially stranger offender, always attract media attention.

From 2001 onwards there were psychology students from the University of Auckland working in our office on rape behaviour theses, naturally under strict provisions and supervision. They were studying statistics and details of offending styles, without being given victims' identities. There were also visits from senior staff from the psychology faculty at Victoria University in Wellington who were using data from our systems in their research.

In addition to attending whodunit homicide cases around the country to provide insights, I was also reviewing cold-case homicides and rapes. Sometimes I would be joined by Lambo for these out-of-town cases, but often I went alone.

Yet another purpose of the unit was to improve all aspects of victim care, throughout both the police investigations and the court process. I believed that how we dealt with and cared for victims of rape was of paramount importance, and good practice would come from educating the staff who dealt directly with them. We lectured on this, and on interviewing, for years.

The unit also took a central role in a number of sexual assault courses, held at the Police College in Porirua. Through Veronica, one of the detectives who had been the liaison officers for our Operation Harvey ladies, we arranged for two of the ladies to attend a number of these courses as speakers. They had experienced a sexual attack, a police investigation and the court process, and had also been interviewed by Jan Jordan for *Serial Survivors*. Jan was also a regular speaker and coordinator at these courses.

These ladies, these victims of rape, may very well have found it difficult to become speakers on sexual assault courses — but they still volunteered to help. From them, course members received first-hand accounts of how victims of sexual assault coped with the different phases of the post-attack experience: first police involvement, medical examination, interview, court and post-court life. Their contributions represent an extraordinary commitment to help others dealing with this process in their professional capacity, and to help those whose own lives might unfortunately lead them down this dark alley. It may, possibly, have also provided an element of catharsis for them.

12. THE POWER OF PROFILING

FROM A PRACTICAL PERSPECTIVE, OUR duties as a squad fell into a number of different categories, but the two main ones were (1) to provide propensity evidence to present in court, and (2) to provide prioritised suspect lists for active cases. We also reviewed cold cases, both rapes and homicides. Time spent increasing the unit's contacts with overseas experts in the field was helpful, as was the knowledge gained at local universities and the time spent educating police staff. (Of course, there were also the mundane monthly updates to prove our worth and therefore ensure our survival.)

PROPENSITY EVIDENCE, OR 'similar facts', is evidence of similar misconduct by a defendant that can be accepted by a court if it is relevant and the judge considers that its value as proof outweighs the prejudicial effect on the defendant. It was rarely, if ever, used in New Zealand courts until the late 1980s, when a more commonsense approach prevailed.

Our propensity evidence was principally based on information in the ViCLAS behavioural database along with the use of statistics to support the evidence; we looked to see how common (or otherwise) a particular behaviour was, to demonstrate how unlikely it would be for the offender to be someone other than the defendant (I give examples of this later in the chapter). The aim was to prevent severance of cases, meaning that they would be tried separately and the evidence would therefore not be as compelling. A pre-trial joinder hearing was held to decide whether the propensity evidence reached the standard required to bring all the similar cases together at one trial. I gave evidence at numerous joinder hearings. Where the propensity evidence was accepted, it often resulted in a guilty plea and a trial was averted. Other times it resulted in the current offences being brought together with previously unsolved cases at one trial. Later in this chapter I describe examples of both these situations. In the case of Rewa, we used propensity evidence to include the case in the 1970s where Rewa was convicted of sexual assault and also bring all our cases together in one trial. I gave this type of propensity evidence a number of times. It became increasingly compelling and persuasive with the inclusion of data from ViCLAS, including international data from overseas ViCLAS systems, which strengthened the statistical element.

PROVIDING PRIORITISED LISTS of suspects relied principally on the Zwaagsi database, with some input from behavioural analysis.

Behavioural analysis and profiling involves a basic understanding of the motivation of fantasy-driven offenders. The idea is that the fantasy-driven signature, or psychodynamics, displayed by the offender at the scene sketches out his personality. Its essence is captured by an expression, rightly or wrongly attributed to Jane Austen from her novel *Sense and Sensibility*: 'It isn't what we say or think that defines us, but what we do.' There's nothing magical or new about this concept; it has just been fine-tuned to suit the purpose of behavioural analysis, particularly regarding rape behaviour.

If there was no power, control, driven fantasy or ritual involved in stranger rapes, they would be not unlike a big rooster jumping on a hen in the coop and then moving on a few minutes later. There is a lot more going on in a rape than what happens in a chicken coop. It is in this extra activity that the offender's 'signature' is found. One of the fundamentals of behavioural analysis is one of the most basic of rules of battle and confrontation: know your enemy. Any army general or All Blacks coach knows this; and so, too, must a detective. Identifying and understanding the fantasies of sex offenders helps us understand them.

Over a century ago, Dr Edmond Locard, a pioneer in forensic science, formulated the principle that every contact leaves a trace — that the perpetrator of a crime will bring something into the crime scene and leave with something from it. Both can be used as forensic evidence. Locard was referring to fingerprints, hair, fibres, paint scratches, blood and the like; DNA was a later element. He also stated that this forensic evidence does not lie and cannot be wholly absent. Only human failure to find it, study it and understand it can diminish its value.

Behavioural analysis adds a further dimension to this principle, by proposing that an offender leaves his personality at the scene.

This is particularly true for psychologically driven crimes such as stranger rape, where the offender's predetermined ritualistic behaviour — his signature — sketches out his personality. If we study his crime, and understand it and the person that created it, this will help to identify him. I followed the same process in behaviourally analysing every file. I had a table with three columns, headed 'Language', 'Sexual behaviour' and 'Violence/Activity'. I would go through each file, noting the behaviours in the relevant column in the order in which they occurred. Comparing these tables of behaviours enabled me to link attacks through their characteristic signatures.

Stranger sexual offenders live a lot of their lives in their own lonely fantasy world, where they have total control. Even if they are caught, most don't, or can't, let anyone else into this world; it would be an invasion into the private space where their life is lived and under their control. When confronted with the request to admit their deviant behaviours, this type of sex offender will often say that they were out of it on drugs and cannot remember the details. It also leads them to plead guilty at court, thus avoiding having to admit to their fantasy-driven behaviours and enabling them to maintain some control. Admitting to a crime in an interview will draw further inquisition, which the stranger rapist does not welcome. Joe Thompson is therefore rarer than most other rapists.

In certain people, fantasies often give birth to violent crime. In addition to physical rape, sex offenders may incorporate fantasy into their ritual behaviours to achieve sexual satisfaction. Sexual fantasies are, of course, not solely played out by rapists; many are played out in legal or consenting relationships. Examples are BDSM (bondage, discipline/domination, submission/sadism, masochism), cross-dressing, and fixations attached to sexual preferences (like being infatuated with breasts, legs, buttocks, etc.). Rapists' fantasies, on the other hand, are played out illegally and often involve violence. What drives them is the need to exert total power and total control.

Where do these fantasies arise? In their early years and experiences. In the early 1980s, Captain John Manning and I attended a rape scene in Hill Park, Manurewa in which a Polynesian youth with a stocking over his head had attacked and raped a woman hanging out her clothes. The description we had was very vague, but fortunately a uniformed senior sergeant in Papakura, 15 kilometres away from the scene, thought a young man getting off a bus fitted the description and took him to the station. Astoundingly, and with ridiculous luck, he was the offender — Nio Paiti.

I had had dealings with Paiti some years earlier, when he was fourteen years old and committing burglaries in Manurewa. At one of these burglaries a school girl was home from school sick, and Paiti dropped his pants and masturbated in front of her, to her disgust. Masturbating in front of this girl while committing the burglary was a telling precursor of later sexual rapes. A few years later, Paiti was convicted of an intruder rape in Manurewa for which he was sentenced to imprisonment at Waikeria. On his release he took a bus to Manurewa, where he got off, walked up the hill and raped our woman hanging out her clothes. This young man's predilection to sexual violence was clearly well established very early in his life. One of his brothers was also convicted of an intruder rape and murder. One can't but wonder what happened in their home when they were young.

I spoke to Paiti in the 1980s in the early hours while on night shift, after recognising him walking down Great South Road. Not up to any mischief, as far as I knew, but I think this is probably the last sighting of him by authorities. When we looked for him during Operation Park he had, strangely, disappeared; there wasn't even a traffic ticket. After I retired I tried to notify him as a missing person — I thought he was probably dead, and someone might dig up his bones sometime in the future — but was told that only a next-of-kin could report someone missing. As you can imagine, I was not pleased with this response!

The source of a sex offender's dangerous power, sense of control, and sexual fantasies differs from person to person. Many blame pornography. In one case I dealt with in Manurewa in 1989, pornography certainly played a part but I doubt it was the source. The offender had been hanging around in a stationery shop, waiting until the other customers had left before attacking and sexually violating the female owner and her daughter. He was identified from a thumbprint on a magazine he'd been looking through while waiting, which had a picture of two blonde women tied back to back, semi-naked — exactly the same way this offender tied up the two blonde women he attacked. I suspect his initial idea was to rob the till, but the pornography took him to another place — his sexual fantasies sourced early in life then inflamed by pornography. The offender never admitted the offences, but was convicted.

Creating the chart of Rewa's signature behaviours for his trial was a great help not only for the trial, but also in that it helped me understand some of the finer points of rape behaviour — and, importantly, identify how certain very particular details were crucial in identifying and linking crimes, and also in eliminating others. The lack of a behaviour — such as the non-involvement of Rewa's victims — is likewise an important element of an offender's behavioural profile.

GEOGRAPHIC PROFILING WAS, of course, another tool in the unit's box. David Canter wrote a second book, *Mapping Murder*, which focused on this aspect of profiling. It includes a chapter on Operation Park that I had some input on. In former FBI agent John Douglas's book *Obsession*, which followed on from *Mindhunter*, he also describes Operation Park in some detail. As I said earlier in this book, following Canter's terminology as the creator of the concept, we classified the Park offender — the Ghost — as a 'marauder offender': someone who ventures out from a given location, his home or a bolt hole, to rape. In Operation Harvey, the Lone Wolf was a different type: what Canter calls a 'commuter rapist'. This type of offender is mobile, and travels to an area with which he is familiar and where his chosen victim types are.

Another example of a commuter rapist is Gary Patrick Brown, a dangerous sociopathic power and control rapist. In 1988 he took a younger gang associate as his driver and went to Middlemore Hospital in South Auckland at 11 p.m., knowing this was the time the nurses and doctors changed shifts; there would be women walking to their cars in the car park. Brown attacked and stabbed a trainee doctor before kidnapping her and taking her to rural South Auckland. After brutally raping and otherwise sexually violating her, he and his young accomplice drove back towards Papakura, discussing the different ways they could dispose of their victim. Burning her in the car was one suggestion, but they settled on driving the car into the Waikato River with her tied up in the back. All through this, the victim was conscious and heard everything. Fortunately, the car got a puncture; while the young offender was fetching a replacement wheel, Brown fell asleep and the victim made her escape. She hid for hours behind a nearby dairy until she was found by the bread delivery man, soon assisted by the night-shift sergeant, just before dawn.

We located the vehicle, which led us to the young driver and a good idea of who the main offender was. After some persuasion the driver confirmed what we already suspected — the identity of the man we wanted most. We knew he was armed and dangerous, and even fellow gang members wanted nothing to do with him — he was too unstable and unpredictable. For several weeks, every sighting or suspected sighting was attended by a member of the Armed Offenders Squad, until eventually Brown was arrested in Hamilton — with a loaded speargun by his bedside. After a tricky trial, he was sentenced to ten years imprisonment.

OVER THE YEARS, we refined our processes and took advantage of advances in forensic techniques to continually improve the service the Criminal Profiling Unit provided to the police — and thus, indirectly, to the public. This largely came about through improving our behavioural analysis, and having a better understanding both of offender type and different types of offending in order to fine-tune our profile. Here, I have selected a cross-section of cases we worked on as a sample of the profiling work we carried out between 2000 and 2007, in an attempt to cover as many aspects of the Criminal Profiling Unit's focus as possible. Many of these cases received national attention.

MURDER OF TERESA CORMACK — OFFENDER NEAR TOP OF PRIORITISED SUSPECT LIST

In June 1987, six-year-old Teresa Cormack was abducted in Napier, Hawke's Bay, then raped and murdered. She was buried in a shallow grave on a pebble beach on the outskirts of the city.

Teresa had left for school that morning wearing a red raincoat and was never again seen alive by anyone but the offender. Her murder naturally caught the public's attention, and the photo of this young girl with her innocent face and her red raincoat haunted the country for many years. It haunted those who tried to find the perpetrator for much longer; this tragic homicide remained unsolved for fifteen years. Teresa's family and others who knew her best would, of course, be haunted forever.

The break came in 2001 when improved DNA processes were able to obtain a profile of the offender's DNA from a very small sample of semen. Although earlier attempts at a DNA profile had been made, at that stage it was too early in the evolution of the science and the attempts failed. Fortunately, unlike in many other crimes, the sample was not completely used up — a small amount had been vacuum-sealed between slides and kept aside for just this development. Great forward thinking both by the officer in charge of the inquiry and those in charge of forensic testing at ESR.

We were approached by the new inquiry head, (the late) Detective Sergeant Brian Schaab, to use Zwaagsi to provide a suspect list for blooding. I was confident we could provide a list that would include the offender, and would be able to prioritise it so that the offender's name was near the top of the list. The basis of this confidence was twofold. First, sexual predators who target young children have the highest recidivism rate of any criminal type. This means they will continue to offend and will also have early 'precursor' crimes involving children. Second, the offender's displayed behaviour clearly indicated that he was experienced at offending against young children, and therefore would have a criminal record of this type of prior offending. He would also have a connection to the Hawke's Bay area, and to Napier in particular.

This level of detail would be valuable in creating our prioritised list of suspects.

Lambo and I travelled to Napier to examine the scene and study the case files, then produced our prioritised list for Schaab. We emphasised to him that the offender would likely be in the top part of the list, and they should concentrate on anyone on the list who became at all evasive, and not skip him to get on with the rest.

The offender, Julius Pierre Mikus, was in the top twenty. He had all the necessary and expected previous offending and would have been number one on the list if only his very early sexual offending against children had been included in his charge data in the Wanganui Computer. Unfortunately, these early convictions pre-dated the Wanganui Computer system which came into service in 1976, and thus were not captured by Zwaagsi.

Still, it was a massive improvement on the Park and Harvey lists of thousands. It helped the murder inquiry team to quickly bring a fifteen-year-old homicide inquiry to a conclusion.

Mikus evaded police for some time, but was arrested in February 2002. He was convicted of the murder of Teresa, whose timid little child's face is as clear in my mind now as it was then. While there is never true closure for the family, we did all we could do, even if we were late achieving it. Mikus remained in prison until his death in September 2019. His next parole hearing had been set for 2020.

OPERATION JAKE
— LINKING UNSOLVED CRIMES TO PRESENT CRIMES

Guido McGlone, who had been a detective with me at Papakura and was involved early in attending the Operation Park scenes, was by 2001 an experienced and established detective sergeant and still working in South Auckland. Among his cases were a couple of rapes that had occurred in Manurewa and Manukau in 1998, which appeared to be linked. The houses of both victims backed on to a bush reserve. The rapes were both daytime intruder attacks where the victims had been tied up in an unusual way, followed by a ritualistic sexual violation. In both cases the attack involved gratuitous degradation of the victims. Operation Jake was put together to investigate the rapes.

One case had been linked by DNA to a man called Tony Albert, who was already in prison for another violent crime. After analysing both rapes, it was clear to me that they had been committed by the same offender. I then searched the Auckland area for any other cold-case rape files that could have been committed by this monster, and found one that had taken place in an entirely different area of Auckland — Ōrākei. The same degrading ritual had been present, together with it having been a daytime rape with the victim tied up in the same unusual way. Without some supporting evidence, however, it wasn't certain to get a guilty verdict at court and I advised the Operation Jake team of this.

During the Ōrākei offence, some property had been stolen and I noted that a distinctive watch was among the items stolen. Finding that would provide strong supporting evidence, and indeed Guido's team found the watch in Albert's possession. He now faced all three rape charges in court.

I viewed Tony Albert's previous offending, and it was alarming and frightening. He had committed numerous intruder offences that had included sexual and control elements: the same shocking degradation and humiliation of his victims. In one attack he had tied up an elderly male, in the same way as he had the three female victims in the rape charges, and had masturbated over him. In my view, Albert was a very dangerous man and, from a sadistic behavioural viewpoint, one of the worst offenders in New Zealand I had read about.

Albert pleaded guilty to the three rape charges. He behaved badly in court and had to be removed from the courtroom when his summary of facts was read out. This behaviour, in my opinion, was contrived by him because he did not want to be present when the summary of his ritual sexual fantasies and sadism was read out in court. It would have been an intrusion into his world that he could not allow.

Tony Albert received a minimum of fourteen years' imprisonment. This was reduced to twelve years on appeal, but he also had a sentence of preventive detention, which was likely to keep him in for much longer. At the time of writing, in 2023, he remains in prison.

TAURANGA HOMICIDE
— A COMBINED CRIMINAL AND GEOGRAPHIC PROFILE

Also in 2001 the profiling team was asked to assist with a homicide in Tauranga. On the surface it appeared to be a stranger attack in the home of an elderly couple, in which the husband was stabbed to death. After entering the house, the offender had taken a knife from the kitchen and stabbed the husband as he rose from his bed to investigate the noise. The knife was left in the victim, and the offender departed the address without a word being spoken.

The location of the house was of interest: it was at the end of a cul-de-sac in an isolated peninsula-type suburb. Both the street and the suburb itself led nowhere. Unless you lived there or knew someone living there, you would have no reason to go there — or even to know it existed. This meant the investigative team had to eliminate the possibility that the victim had been targeted. There was some support for this theory. First, a person with the same or a similar name had just been convicted and named in the media for sexual offending against children. Second, the victim had worked as a supervisor at the Tauranga Periodic Detention Centre, where offenders completed supervised community work as part of their court sentence.

While both of these could possibly have made the victim a target, these theories seemed unlikely to me. A visit to the scene showed clearly that this was a disorganised crime, one that showed no evidence of planning. The offender had used a weapon from the victim's house, then left it behind (in the victim). He had made no attempt to disguise himself and made no comment that would indicate a reason for the attack. In my view, the victim had not been targeted, but instead had fallen prey to an offender who could be suffering from a psychiatric illness or experiencing a psychotic event.

The big question was what had brought the offender to this isolated location in this isolated suburb? It was likely that there was a link to the area somewhere in his past. It was an opportunity to use Zwaagsi to try to find that link. The wife, who had witnessed the homicide, provided a useful description of the offender. First up, she described the offender's very shiny bald head, emphasising the shiny aspect. Next, she thought he was about the same age as her son. This was important — when someone can relate a description to someone they know, or a place or thing they know, the piece of descriptive evidence is stronger than just a vague idea or an estimate.

Armed with this description, along with the probability of a connection to the area, we turned to Zwaagsi to produce a profile. In the meantime, the Tauranga detectives identified the offender themselves from other evidence. It turned out that he had alopecia, hence his shiny head. And he was within a year of the age provided by the victim's wife. Zwaagsi showed that he had one 'convicted and discharged' entry for wilful damage, which had taken place when, for a short time, he had lived one street away from the victim's house as a teenager; over a decade earlier.

The offender was now living in South Auckland, and we assisted the Tauranga detectives in arresting him. He had no rational reason for being at the victim's house and did not know him. He had simply walked to the house at the end of the cul-de-sac, entered through a window and stabbed the victim for no reason. This was what is known as a random stranger homicide.

What we drew from this investigation was that Zwaagsi was indeed a valuable investigative tool, even if it was not directly responsible for this particular offender's identification and arrest.

SERIAL RAPIST NICHOLAS REEKIE — USE OF PROPENSITY EVIDENCE

This serial rapist operating around Auckland, particularly in the west, was a very sexually confused individual who presented a dynamic sexual behaviour — his victims ranged from prepubescent children in bed in their homes to a 69-year-old woman living in a retirement home, as well as 23- and 24-year-old women walking innocently in the street. At first glance there didn't seem to be a lot to link the crimes either behaviourally or chronologically — some occurred a decade after previous ones. But on deeper analysis, all of the cases displayed some telling ritualistic and unusual behaviours that linked them together into a series.

One of the cases also involved an infamous miscarriage of justice with regard to David Dougherty, who had been convicted for the intruder abduction rape of an eleven-year-old West Auckland girl taken from her bed. He was her next-door neighbour and was identified incorrectly by the victim as the offender. Dougherty was later pardoned after DNA testing revealed that the crime had been committed by someone else.

DNA evidence led to Nicholas Reekie being arrested in 2002 and charged with several abduction and rape offences. Although there were obvious differences in scene type, ages of victims and chronology, we analysed the files for behavioural similarities to see whether we could tie various cases together and link them with one of the attacks on children for which Reekie had been already convicted a decade earlier.

To explain what 'behavioural similarities' means, I use a favourite analogy. If I were to remove the cover and title pages from a book by one of your favourite authors that you hadn't yet read, you might well be able to identify the author from the genre and the writing style, regardless of the plot. When you apply behavioural analysis methodology to a number of rapes committed by one offender, the same is true: the same theme (genre) and style are present throughout. Even if the apparent 'plots' are completely different, with experience you can quickly recognise if you have previously 'read' this person.

Reekie's was such a case. While he might appear to be committing a totally different type of offence (a different plot), his style was glaring out at us. I gave evidence of these similarities at a pre-trial joinder hearing. The defence wanted severance so that each victim's case would have to stand alone without the support of corroborating evidence offered by the other victims, therefore weakening the Crown's case.

However, we were able to tie the cases together. We did this by showing that while one or two of them were clearly linked to the one he had been previously convicted for, others were not so obviously linked. *But:* these other cases were clearly linked to the one or two cases which *were* linked, so therefore they all knitted together. It was a classic propensity case. I produced one of my charts showing all the links. It was important to have all the cases with similar offender behavioural patterns heard together, as this powerfully demonstrates to a jury that the similarities could not possibly be due to a coincidence, or be made up by any of the victims.

Justice Fisher, who had sentenced Joseph Thompson and was considered a bit of a guru when it came to propensity evidence, presided over this joinder hearing and dismissed the defence's application for severance. In other words, he judged that there was significant commonality in all the cases to accept the propensity evidence. In earlier years, propensity evidence did not carry much weight, if any, in court. There also seemed to be little effort made by the Crown or other prosecutors to push the case for similar facts to be recognised and tried. But after Operation Harvey there was a groundswell of acceptance in the courts.

After the subsequent trial, Reekie received a minimum of 25 years' imprisonment, later reduced to twenty years. The sentencing judge (not Justice Fisher) commented that Reekie was probably beyond rehabilitation and had a deep-seated psychosis. Although Reekie responded with tears, he was considered to have demonstrated a profound lack of remorse. In an attempt to project blame, he claimed that it was the prison's fault for releasing him too soon after his previous conviction. Reekie was declined parole in 2022 and remains in prison at the time of writing.

CHRISTIAN BRUSEY
— USE OF BEHAVIOURAL LINKAGE AND PROPENSITY EVIDENCE

This case is a salutary lesson for those who may still believe that castration prevents further sexual offending. It highlights the issue that a sex offender's problem is between his ears and not between his legs.

Brusey committed numerous intruder sexual attacks in Wellington in the early 2000s. This criminal had a personal history and behaviour that would make a grand study for any psychologist or psychiatrist. He had been adopted into a wealthy and influential family in Wellington as a three-year-old. When his adoptive parents picked him up, he reportedly said, 'Are you going to be my mother and father now?' On the face of it this might seem an innocent, even lovely, sentiment, but — in hindsight — I think it had a very sinister overture, especially the word 'now'. It shows that despite his young age, he probably had already had other adoptive parents who had abandoned him, or he had moved in and out of welfare establishments and fostering.

Brusey's adoptive parents were Europeans in their forties, who adopted children of colour. Brusey and his biological brother whom the couple also adopted were now in a home where the parents had busy lives and were people of standing in the Wellington community. The boys were sent to boarding school out of town. I believe that Brusey had already developed issues with abandonment, which may have been reinforced by the boarding situation. Abandonment and neglect prior to seven years of age were common factors in the childhood histories of the serial rapists and murderers I profiled. He might also have been 'born bad', as a judge told him at a sentencing. Most likely it was a combination of both; we will never know. Either way, he progressed to a life of drugs, crime and sexual offending.

His alleged inheritance of over $1 million on his parents' deaths, together with what should have been a good-quality education, clearly had little effect on his behaviour.

What we do know is that being brought up in a large home in an affluent part of the city influenced the types of homes Brusey offended in during his series of intruder sexual attacks. Joe Thompson attacked predominantly young Pasifika and Māori girls in lower-socioeconomic areas of South Auckland, which were familiar to him and where he felt comfortable. Brusey attacked middle-aged European women, like his adoptive mother, in wealthy suburbs in large homes; likewise familiar to him and where he felt comfortable.

By the early 2000s, Brusey was a serious drug user and an experienced criminal, with over 200 previous convictions acquired during a 30-year career in crime. Most people working in the criminal industry in Wellington from the early '70s onwards — on both sides of the law — will know of Brusey.

He appeared to have major erectile dysfunction, possibly due to his drug use; this likely affected his sexual activities during attacks. Brusey entered houses in the early hours and always tied his female victims to the bed. He then carried out his sexual fetish, which always had a vaginal theme but never involved the use of his penis. There was a ritual element too, involving sadistic violence with a clear intent to degrade the victims.

Erectile dysfunction is not uncommon with stranger intruder rapists. Many people believe that these rapists are motivated by sexual arousal — lust — or sexual frustration, but the erectile dysfunction actually shows that it is all about power and control, not sexual pleasure. There are plenty of examples in the research where rapists have no problem with sexual dysfunction during consensual sex but do when committing rape. The problem lies in disordered thinking rather than a disordered body.

By November 2003, Detective Sergeant Leitch and his team had put together a good case against Brusey for a number of intruder sexual offences in Wellington. We at the Criminal Profiling Unit now needed to sew them together. Our analysis highlighted a strong behavioural theme. Again I gave evidence at a pre-trial joinder hearing in the High Court in Wellington aimed at having all the attacks heard together at one trial. The request for severance put forward by the defence was denied.

After this hearing, Brusey pleaded guilty to all nineteen serious charges — rather than face a trial and have his sexual fetishes and deviancy exposed in more detail. On a positive note, this also meant all his victims were saved the trauma of reliving their horrific experiences. Brusey was sentenced to preventive detention on 5 September 2005, with Justice David Gendall commenting on his lack of remorse and escalating sexual violence. The judge's summing-up emphasised the whole point of 'similar fact' evidence at joinder hearings — to encourage the defence to consider a guilty plea and therefore spare the victims the trauma of having to give evidence.

Brusey is still in custody as I'm writing this book, nearly twenty years later.

JUSTIN AMES JOHNSTON — LINKING OF COLD CASE

In 2003/2004 Lambo found an unsolved rape file dating back to 1994 that he thought dovetailed with a rape that had taken place nearby only a year later. Justin Johnston had been prosecuted and convicted for the later offence. On analysis, I found that the general behaviour and facts of the cases were indeed very similar. Both attacks were committed in the same suburb, 2 kilometres apart, by a lone stranger who gained entry through a downstairs window in the early hours of the morning while the victims, both young Caucasian women, were asleep in bed. The initial attack was surprise style, with the offender, who wore a balaclava, placing his hand over the victim's mouth and telling her to be quiet, before gagging and blindfolding her with duct tape and cloth ties he had brought with him.

The verbal behaviour at both scenes also had similarities. The offender reassured the victim that he was not going to hurt her. He told her he had girlfriends and provided personal and employment details (all lies, of course), and asked her about her sexual history and practices. He also said that he wasn't good-looking and had acne. Both victims described the offender as being Caucasian with brown hair, wearing a necklace and smelling of alcohol. When the victim refused to perform sexual acts as he'd requested, he continued with other sexual activity. After finishing, he extended the time spent with the victim by having a drink and a cigarette while talking to them, then left.

Justin Johnston had acne, and lived just over a kilometre from the rape for which he'd been convicted and around 400 metres from the unsolved case. A stolen car was abandoned around a kilometre from each scene; in the proved case this was around 3 kilometres from Johnston's home and in the unsolved case just 400 metres.

While many of these similarities were modus operandi, and therefore not as compelling, others were much rarer and went directly to his signature and ritual behaviours. To find these in two cases so closely positioned chronologically and geographically was compelling.

The matter was brought in front of the court as Johnston was due for parole for the attack he had been convicted for in 1995. We succeeded in getting him convicted for the earlier crime and he remained in custody for a further period of imprisonment. This also brought resolution for the victim of the earlier offence. Without behavioural analysis evidence put before the court, and the more open view towards propensity evidence, this earlier case would never have made its way into court — let alone have brought about a conviction.

On his release, Johnston was again convicted of a sexual offence after having been spotted outside a young woman's residence. The court judgment in this case included a psychiatrist's description of an anti-social or psychopathic personality disorder, with offending patterns offering little chance of rehabilitation. Johnston received preventive detention. At parole hearings in 2016 and 2022, parole was declined.

BRENT MCLENNAN — BEHAVIOURAL LINKAGE

In 2006 we were asked to assist Detective Sergeant Mike Bowman with a couple of stranger street rapes in Invercargill. Mike was keen to have both cases heard together in court, to provide support for each case evidentially as well as emotionally, with the ultimate aim of getting as many of the facts before the jury as legally possible to help them convict the guilty party and, hopefully, eliminate the need for the victims to go through a harrowing court process.

In Justice Phillips' judgment he recognised the depth of experience I had in analysing behavioural characteristics in various types of offending, saying that in his view I was quite clearly an expert in the analysis of behaviour in sexually motivated crimes. In this case, while there were similarities in the modus operandi of the two crimes, the ritualistic aspects formed the strongest links. Not only was the sexual behaviour very distinctive, involving objects being placed in the victim's anus, but in both cases passports and other personal identifying items ('souvenirs') were also taken by the offender. These were the only items stolen, and the similarity between them would have been astonishing should the cases not be linked to one offender.

McLennan's lawyer spent some time cross-examining me. One point that came up several times was the offender's focus on the anus. Although different objects had been used, Justice Phillips accepted my statement that the placing of objects in the anus is extremely rare, and the nature of the object was not the issue; the theme — the anal focus itself — spoke to the theme of the offender's behaviour. Justice Phillips summed up my evidence-giving as follows:

> In all, despite the close questioning, Detective Sergeant
> Henwood did not in my view change his opinion in relation
> to both the specific ritualistic behaviours and the general
> commonality being in this particular set of circumstances
> described by him as 'extraordinary'.
>
> I have considered all the evidence given by Detective
> Sergeant Henwood. I accept from his evidence that there are
> compelling specific and general behaviours displayed during
> these two attacks.
>
> . . . The evidence on one is clearly relevant to the other.

For this case, we had combined our ViCLAS database with that of the UK's Serious Crime Analysis Section for a statistical analysis of the commonality of the behaviours displayed by the rapist. Out of the total of 100,002 cases we examined there was not one case in which all the elements listed in the table I'd prepared were present in combination — as they were in the assaults on the two victims in the current cases.

Once the two attacks had been linked to the same offender, so would be heard together, the defendant pleaded guilty to both attacks and the victims avoided going through a trial. In March 2007, McLennan was sentenced to fourteen years of imprisonment with a minimum non-parole period of seven years. At his parole hearing in 2016, McLennan was assessed as a high risk of further sexual offending and parole was declined. The parole board's report refers to him having entitlement attitudes, minimum insight and being inclined to brood on perceived wrongdoing towards him by female staff. The end date for his sentence was in 2019, regardless of parole. As far as I know, he was released; I have heard nothing more.

ROGER TIRA KAHUI
— BUILDING A MEANINGFUL AND MANAGEABLE
PRIORITISED SUSPECT LIST

In 2006, a chilling, brutal rape and abduction took place in Pukekohe. The offender forced his way into a woman's home. After punching her, he raped her numerous times and committed other sexual offences against her in a four-and-a-half-hour ordeal. He also forced her to watch a pornographic film. He then forced her into her car and took her to an ATM machine; here he demanded her PIN, telling her that if it was incorrect, he would kill her.

When he stopped the car, despite her hands being cuffed, she managed to escape and run to a service station, where she alerted police.

We were asked to produce a suspect list from a criminal and geographic profile. At the unit we had been improving in every facet of our work, including interviewing — which provides much of the basis for the investigation. This attack gave us the best possible opportunity — the complainant/victim was articulate, and Mog assisted with conducting the interview, ensuring that the key points were covered appropriately. The result was an accurate profile that provided a perfect geographic and behavioural picture of the offender. Along with a description, we predicted that he probably lived in the vicinity of the victim and had family in the area. He was likely to have a previous conviction for burglary, and perhaps also for peeping.

The O/C for this investigation was Detective Senior Sergeant Neil Grimstone (who had been O/C Scene for the Susan Burdett homicide and also did not believe that Teina Pora had been involved). His recollection of this case is recorded in John Lockyer's 2010 book *New Zealand Detectives* (p. 226).

> We didn't have a lot to go on, so I talked to Chook — Dave Henwood — who'd been developing a successful criminal profiling system. His team came on board. They listened to the victim's interview, particularly her descriptions of the offender and his actions. From that they compiled a profile and a list of about 120 possible suspects. I said, 'Chook, can you narrow the list down a bit?'
>
> He did. Then I said, 'Are you able to rank the suspects in priority order?'
>
> He did that, too. He gave us a top 20. We put the names through the database. Any suspect that came up without a DNA sample had to be found. A team located each one,

interviewed them, got some blood, then went on to check their alibis. In the meantime, the blood samples were sent to ESR.

A week or so later, about eight at night, a scientist rang me at home. They'd matched the DNA found at the scene to one of the top 20 suspects. The name didn't mean anything to me, so I jumped in the car and went into work. I opened the file, and there was the name. At the top of the list. Number one!

The local police did not know that this offender, Roger Kahui, was living in Pukekohe, in a sleepout in the back of a family property near the victim's house — but his past and his behaviour were responsible for him being caught, just like Joe Thompson. As well as the history we'd predicted, he had a previous conviction for rape.

In January 2009, Kahui was charged and convicted of four rapes, seven unlawful sexual connections, seven indecent assaults, three threatening to kill, two assaults, one injuring with intent, one aggravated burglary, and one kidnapping — all relating to the same complainant. Justice Williams sentenced him to preventive detention. In 2021, Kahui's parole application was declined.

Kahui's capture and conviction was a thrill for the Criminal Profiling Unit. What was special about this case was that we had identified the most likely offender with such a high level of accuracy — instead of thousands of names on the suspect list we had only twenty, and the offender was right at the top, at number one. Using Zwaagsi and ViCLAS had enabled us to develop the perfect offender profile and thus a crucial investigative tool. This was significant progress.

13. THE END OF
THE BEGINNING

AS I APPROACHED 55 YEARS of age, the Criminal Profiling Unit — now with a staff of three, plus me as O/C, to cover the whole country — was experiencing considerable success. The extra staff member was Dave Scott, who was part-way through a doctorate in psychology. He added a theoretical and academic edge to the team, which was very different from the practical evidential focus I had experienced in my career in the police department.

However, as much as I enjoyed the work, after a hectic ten years of battling not only criminals but (more frustratingly by far, for me) also the administration, I needed some respite from what had started in February 1993 with the beginning of Operation Park, and led to fifteen years of dealing with rape cases and trying to unmask monsters. The few outstanding historical cases that remained unsolved continued to itch at me, but I could see no way of taking those forward. They would remain open and unsolved.

The administration side of my job was consuming increasing amounts of my time. Time that I would have preferred to have devoted to preparing profiles, attending scenes, lecturing at the Police College and elsewhere, preparing briefs of evidence, attending court battles, keeping the two computer systems moving forward, running the office, and general practical work. I chafed at being distracted by preparing budgets, three-month, six-month and annual projections on where the staff and squad would be, as well as dealing with overtime issues, appraisals on staff and myself and the squad and, most irritating of all, meaningless meetings. This dark place for me was, of course, a fundamental responsibility that came with running the unit.

The unit itself was doing well. I had successfully given evidence on numerous occasions using behavioural analysis. Mog was now also giving evidence in court as an expert, using data sourced from ViCLAS. Zwaagsi was working well under Lambo's eye and our lectures at police training college and around the country continued to be well received. We had an excellent relationship with those in the trenches in all locations, and excellent support from Sue V and the team at ESR.

Perhaps it was battle fatigue, perhaps it was the beckoning of new horizons, but I made up my mind to retire as a sworn officer. I did this in April 2007 — 37 years and three months after arriving at Trentham. Detective Sergeant Brett Pakenham had recently returned from the war crimes tribunal in The Hague and fitted the bill as a practised and smart South Auckland detective to take my place. Although it might have been the beginning of the end for me, it was only the end of the beginning for the unit.

AFTER TEN MONTHS out, which included some travel, I looked around for a job that would be both meaningful and also pay a reasonable salary. I finally did what I had vowed I wouldn't, and that was to return as a non-sworn member of the police. There were a few new roles available in a project called CJSU (Criminal Justice Support Unit). The money seemed reasonable, and I was assured by others of what the job entailed — and, more importantly, what it did not.

Others asked why I didn't return to some sort of consultancy role with the police in the profiling and rape behavioural area. But my goal had always been to do something completely different. I did not want to return to what I had left, and certainly not in the profiling squad — this would not have been fair on Brett Pakenham who was now putting his mark on the job. I felt like I should explore something fresh, even though I still had a strong interest in the area of criminal profiling and rape victims, which continues to this day. In any case, I was never offered such a role.

Thus I joined my old crime car mate Ray 'Spud' Smith in the CJSU, which was set up to take preparation for court cases off the frontline police as much as possible, so they could get on and police the streets without being tied to a computer. That was the theory, anyway, and it had a sound basis, but I was instantly concerned that the work had the potential to create a 'lock them up, walk away' police officer.

It also ran the risk of frontline police losing a vital connection with victims. So much is learnt from going through the court process with regard to crime-scene examination, the potential (or otherwise) of exhibits, interviewing, dealing with the court and defence lawyers, and looking after your victims. We learnt from our mistakes, from things we shouldn't have done and therefore wouldn't do again in the potentially embarrassing environment of a court. Going through this process is how an investigator learns and develops. I wondered how not experiencing this could be a positive thing for police staff development. However, I was advised that a significant component of the CJSU role would involve training new staff and taking them under our wing. It was this that drew me to the position. If the training was carried out in the right way, it would override my reservations.

In this new role, I learnt how much the frontline staff's job had changed since I had been engaged in it many years earlier. It was clearly much more complex. To respond to these changes, it seemed there were now many more highly important tasks than simply catching bad guys. The police now appeared to have a much broader scope of responsibilities, especially in the sociocultural context. Over the previous decade I had been so involved with dealing with rapists and victims of rape that I had not been aware of this development.

Along with the criminal fraternity, the police staff had changed in gender, race, skills, work ethic and reasons for making their career choice. Some changes were necessary and had been long overdue — particularly with regard to ensuring more diverse ethnic and gender representation; I was less convinced about some other factors. In this new world, the general function of policing had changed. Hunting for and locking up criminals was no longer the first priority. Police were becoming social workers involved in every facet of social issues.

I was not opposed to some of the changes, but such a massive directional move brings with it some costly losses. Many were forced on to the police because of a lack of resources for anyone else to deal with issues that now fell to the police. Rather than simply protecting the public from criminal activity, it had become a social service. And given not only the typically meagre staff resources but also a rapid turnover of personnel — perhaps unsurprisingly, due to the pressure — it was a stretch to cover these additional duties. Convicting a culprit was no longer top of the page, or even in the front room. Instead, we seemed hell-bent on keeping as many villains out of prison as we could.

How could we teach new staff the most important lessons arising from our experience when the turnover was so great and the number of new staff unrelenting? The answer was soon forthcoming: we couldn't. From early on I could see that my original reservations were becoming a reality. We constantly had to remember that we were dealing with mainly very inexperienced officers, and now these men and women were in a completely different environment. Changes were inevitable and we needed to move with them, even if we might not agree with all of them.

Although the CJSU started out with much fanfare — the latest grand idea on the block, with lots of staff and even the training role running reasonably well — it didn't last. After a while we lost staff who were not replaced. Others were centralised (the normal government or police way of saving money) as the CJSU was watered down, reviewed and overtaken by the next exciting new idea. The training element of the CJSU was minimalised to almost zero as staff who were to be trained by us could not be spared. In my view, the front line generally became less and less involved in the practice of crime-scene assessment, criminal investigation and the court process — as I had originally suspected they would. Obviously, I felt very out of step with the new direction in the police — the movement away from what I saw as their prime duty, to investigate crime and protect the public. Increasingly, staff were being deployed to pat old ladies on the head and promise what they could no longer provide, because the very staff doing the patting of heads had been taken from the front line. Perhaps that is the way it is meant to be as each generation gives way to the next. Dan the burglar discovered this on his last visit to The Grey Lady (Mt Eden) in the early '90s. I didn't want to be sitting around moaning about the 'new ways'. Change is always around the next corner, of course, but this time I didn't want to be part of it. It seemed like only yesterday that some of the old coppers were whingeing about everything going to the dogs, while I was thinking they should push off and not denigrate the job we were looking forward to embarking on in the new world of the early '70s.

This, as every generation comes to know, is simply the changing of the guard and has to be accepted. But surely we are permitted to agonise over some things that have been lost during the passing of the baton?

I decided to retire when my last mortgage payment had been made. That would make it over 47 years since I had first arrived at Trentham. In the meantime, the great people in the team and the excellent humour kept me reasonably content.

ADDING TO MY frustrations with the job at the CJSU was some history rearing up and causing controversy. The case of Teina Pora had surfaced again, as I had always known it would. It brought me into a direct collision course with the police department for whom I still worked.

My view that Rewa was a lone wolf and Pora was never present at Susan Burdett's murder scene had not altered. The police hierarchy's refusal to revisit and review this case, and the possibility that Pora was innocent of the crime of which he had been convicted, was very disappointing. This, of course, also meant that while Pora remained convicted of the crime, Rewa could never be rightfully convicted of it. It fuelled my desire to quit.

14. JUSTICE FOR TEINA PORA — AND SUSAN BURDETT

IT'S NOT OVER TILL IT'S over.

The case of Teina Pora was a mess; many of us knew it would not just disappear. Analysis of Rewa's behaviour had made it clear to me that Pora could not have been there. Others agreed, though for different reasons, based on the interview with Pora and the lack of a linkage between him and Rewa.

In 2011, when the matter resurfaced, Pora had been in prison since 1993 with a short period of freedom in 1999–2000 for a retrial. Despite my evidence about Rewa's 'distinctive mode of offending' being cited as part of the grounds for ordering the retrial, it was not presented at Pora's second trial, which relied heavily on his confession, and Pora was reconvicted. I was contacted early in 2011 by ex-detective Tim McKinnel, now a private investigator. I figured that as a young detective, he'd remembered the heated discussions at Harlech House and in the Ōtāhuhu police bar regarding the merits of this prosecution and conviction. Tim was now working with Pora, convinced that his case represented a miscarriage of justice. I was relieved to discover that someone had finally picked this up to run with it; it wasn't something I could do from inside the police.

Tim had obtained the services of lawyer Jonathan Krebs, who apparently had been Crown Counsel in Hawke's Bay years earlier. In late March, Krebs asked me to meet him at a coffee shop near the CJSU office to discuss the matter. The bottom line was that he wanted to use my propensity evidence and known views regarding Pora's non-involvement to obtain a pardon for Pora. He particularly wanted to use my evidence around the unlikelihood of Rewa taking Pora to any rape or murder scene.

I told him I would not provide him with a statement along the lines he wanted as these were available to him from my evidence at Rewa's first trial in 1998. What concerned me most was that if I was put up as an expert and then attacked as such by the Crown, it would provide a glimmer of hope and thus a window of opportunity for barrister Barry Hart and Rewa to demand a retrial. There were also the many other cases for which I had given expert evidence in courts around the country — if the Crown attacked their own expert, this could open up a Pandora's box.

Krebs also had concerns regarding the refusal of the police to provide documents from the case. He was willing to receive the victim statements with the detail of the victims removed; he said he already had the basic details from barrister Marie Dyhrberg, who had defended Pora at both of his trials. But he claimed the police had advised him they did not have a copy of the chart of behaviours I'd drawn up. Krebs had already approached barrister Barry Hart because he knew Hart had a lot of the file content —

including the chart — but Krebs decided in the end he'd get it from an alternative source.

Krebs asked if I was aware of some critically flawed processes in the Pora case regarding identification and interviewing techniques. While I was aware of some rumours around this, I refused to look over documents or the interview because I simply did not want to have anything affect my views, which were based solely on the behavioural psychodynamics of Rewa. I did not wish to have this clear and singular view muddied or fudged with other issues that may or may not have existed.

I made it clear to Krebs that I was not involved in any way in the original arrest or any prosecution of Pora, and that I believed Pora's non-involvement in the Burdett homicide had been argued strongly by Mitford, Lambo, Karl and myself both before and after Rewa's trial. The Crown's case at Rewa's trial had been that Mongrel Mob members were involved and also that there was only a tenuous association between Pora and Rewa. The result, of course, was that Rewa was not convicted of the rape or murder of Susan Burdett at his original trial, and only convicted of the rape at his second trial — because the police had not cut him free from association with Pora.

Coming away from this meeting, I had the overwhelming feeling that by continuing to justify a mistake made many years earlier, the police were jeopardising much more. By trying to sticky-tape over Pora, we had already, seemingly, lost any chance of a murder conviction against Rewa. By continuing in this manner, and by not being transparent and refusing certain disclosures, the police would be castigated when the dust finally settled — as it undoubtedly would. The police are meant to be the bearers of the truth.

The solution, it seemed to me and to many others, was to have the case reviewed by an independent police officer who was not tainted by having been involved in either the Pora or Rewa investigations. Based on the evidence, I felt that such a review would conclude that Pora was never at Susan Burdett's home. Another advantage of an internal police review was that officers were more likely to be forthright, open, and legally on solid ground in responding to such an inquiry. They would be less likely to confidently express their knowledge and views to someone outside the police, such as Tim McKinnel, Jonathan Krebs, or their team.

I am far from a tree-hugging believer in the innocence of many thieves, thugs and psychopaths who regularly claim such innocence. But I am aware that some innocent men and women can find themselves behind bars.

IN JANUARY 2012, Tim McKinnel made a formal request for a statement from me. I told him I'd call him back after I had sought guidance from a senior officer involved with the Pora file. I needed to check out the legality of making statements about what I had learnt while a sworn member of the police, especially given that I was still employed by the police, albeit in a non-sworn capacity.

The answer: sensitive information obtained within fiduciary relationships should not be divulged, except in certain environments such as a court. There was a further legal view that if the interests of justice were to be served by it being disclosed, then it should be. Also, because I was no longer a sworn member of the police, they had no hold over me making a statement in general terms about anything, perhaps with the exception of the first point made.

It was clearly a minefield. Looking back, perhaps that's what was intended by communicating this to me. I advised the senior officer I would not be making a statement to Tim McKinnel.

The following month, I was summonsed to the High Court with a direction to produce my crime chart and other charts from Operation Harvey. I advised the officer of this summons; his terse response was that the chart belonged to the police, not me. If I had a copy of the chart (I did not), I was to return it to him. I was also not permitted to enter the Criminal Profiling Unit office to view a copy held there or to view the one on the wall. This last was a reference to my large crime chart used at the Rewa trial, which covered an entire wall in my old CPU office — now Brett Pakenham's.

I knew that Krebs and McKinnel could easily acquire a copy of the chart from other sources. Refusing to provide one would not be in the police's best interest, or that of justice. Meanwhile, I was between a rock and a hard place — I had a court order in the form of a summons to attend court and produce a chart I had prepared years earlier while a sworn officer, and the police refused me the right to access it or produce it. I contacted the Police Association to provide me with a lawyer. On the day of the court case, however, I was advised that the matter had been settled out of court. I was never told — by either side — about what took place and how it was resolved. Regardless, I knew this was far from the end of the legal charade surrounding Pora and Rewa.

As the matter simmered on, I made it clear to the senior officer what the consequences would be if my credibility was undermined — that should my expert opinion be attacked, it would weaken my 'expert' evidence given nationally with regard to numerous other sexual offenders then in prison. It could also undermine the Criminal Profiling Unit and its impact on future cases. His stance, and that of the police hierarchy, was that two juries had found Pora guilty and that was where it would stay.

It was clear to me that, in the end, the police would be castigated over some of the issues arising from the Pora prosecution. A little harm reduction from being clear and open now would surely lessen the amount of blood spilt on the floor and the damage to the police's public image. That was my view, and the reason behind what happened next.

MCKINNEL AND KREBS'S investigation continued to gather momentum. I knew in my gut what the final outcome would, and should, be. Many agreed with me, but were side lined by the lack of appetite for an internal police review of the evidence.

In May 2012, out of the blue, Phil Taylor rang me. He was a journalist with whom I had had dealings in connection with burglar Dan Dudson many years earlier. Phil had also reported on the Operation Park and Harvey court cases and investigations. He was one of the few journalists I trusted — not some shallow penman looking for a sensational story to sell a newspaper or to rate well on TV. Most journalists, it seems, are in a rush to be the first to get a story out. Unfortunately, justice and the law operate at a much slower pace. It may take months to source the real truth — or at least most of it. And, of course, the *real* truth three months later is not a front-page story, as the initial report might have been. This can put the media on a different track and with a different goal to that sought by police.

Phil is a true investigative journalist who was excited by, and on the lookout for, big meaningful stories and the truth behind them. He'd deduced from my evidence at the first Rewa trial, where I'd said, 'If indeed there was anyone else present', that I did not believe Pora was involved with the attack on Susan Burdett. Defence counsel Barry Hart had not expanded on this during the trial. Either he missed its relevance, or he chose to avoid what he suspected was a minefield that might not help his client. Almost no one else seemed to have picked up on this. Phil also knew of Tim's crusade to free Pora.

Straight away, Phil asked me if I believed that Pora was present with Rewa at the Susan Burdett murder and rape scene. A simple question. Should I go out on a limb and answer it?

Ringing in my ears were comments made by Bruce (the police chaplain) and reinforced by the then Minister of Police very recently at the opening of the new Ormiston police station, about the police's role in the community: they spoke of 'prosecuting the guilty and vindicating the innocent'. I thought, well, let's just see whether 'vindicating the innocent' are words with real meaning or just shallow rhetoric. I figured that I had held my breath on this one too long already. I had received no thanks for this, either.

I knew what I was about to say would bring me into the direct line of fire from a number of angles. But what was the worst they could do? Sack me, fine me, growl at me? I thought I could take that, though some of my old mates would probably not agree with the course of action I took, and I understood that too.

My response to Phil was direct, and clearly explosive.

'I believe Rewa committed the crime alone and that Pora was innocent. You have a joker (Rewa) who is not convicted of murdering Susan Burdett, who did murder her, and the reason he is not convicted of it is because Pora is in the road. It is one that has stuck in the craw and there are no doubts in my mind.'

I think Phil was surprised at how direct my response was. He had probably expected some sort of fudging around the issue.

And, of course, my unequivocal statement hit the front page of the newspaper: 'Innocent man in jail 20 years'.

I was now in 'a little bit of trouble' with my employer. Had I not been employed by the police, I could have said whatever I wanted without any repercussions. But repercussions there would be.

I was surprised, though, when (the late) Tim Smith, a fellow ex-detective senior sergeant from South Auckland, chimed in with his support. Unbeknownst to me, he had been on the original inquiry in April to June 1992 when Pora was first considered and then dismissed as a suspect. I hadn't known that Tim held these views. He was present again during Pora's confessions in March 1993, made on video to Ruthers and Mark Williams. From the outset, Tim had believed the confessions were false and Pora was never at the Susan Burdett murder scene. What's more, he had expressed these beliefs at the time.

After the exposé of my beliefs appeared in the paper, Tim emailed the Commissioner of Police telling him that he agreed totally with my views and asked for the case to be urgently reviewed. This didn't happen. What we did get, however, was permission from the Commissioner to make statements to McKinnel and Krebs, which of course we both did.

What struck me most, afterwards, was the number of experienced detectives who had been involved in many aspects of the Pora investigation and who held the same views as me. I hadn't previously known this because I had never worked on any part of the investigation into Pora. The general feeling from most of these detectives was that Pora was just a silly boy mouthing off. My own view!

I received a lot of support from other detectives I respected. The sheer number of senior detectives voicing their concern was not something I had seen before when someone had become a whistle-blower against the police. But there was also discontent. Words like 'traitor' popped up, mainly from those who knew little to nothing of the case first-hand and from those who had never been in the trenches with me.

I spoke with Greg O'Connor, president of the New Zealand Police Association, to advise him of what I saw as the dangers the police were heading towards. I know he spoke with others who held similar views to me, though I had not sent him in their direction as they were not hard to find. The result was that the Police Association asked for an internal police inquiry into Pora. Just as I had, Greg got himself into hot water over his request. He nearly lost his position with the association because of members who perhaps saw his request as a betrayal. But he was a powerful figure and managed to hold off the voices of ignorance. On his retirement in 2016, Greg commented in the Police Association's newsletter *Police News*: 'It was a hard thing for the Association to do — to come out and say he was innocent. We had been sitting on the sidelines, but it was clear that something had gone wrong . . . Lessons have to be learnt. Every organisation goes through that.'

Unfortunately, Greg's request — just like Tim Smith's and mine — brought no change in stance from the police hierarchy in Wellington, and the matter continued to garner bad press for the police. The hierarchy appeared to be willing to go along with the previous court result, regardless of the evidence and, particularly, of the growing number of staff within the police who wanted the evidence re-examined. Legal precedence and political input perhaps also played a part in this intransigent position.

Eventually, once the slow wheels of the police investigation into my 'news release' had ground to a halt, I was 'growled' at by the

Police Professional Standards Office and counselled for speaking out in breach of police regulations. The first black mark on my personal record since Ted and I had purchased the beer at Totara Lodge 43 years earlier. Present were the district commander, the professional standards inspector, Stew Mills for the association, and me. I admitted I had broken the rules. I told the district commander and the inspector, 'I know where this will end up, and what I have said and been counselled for here might be the only shining light for the police as it plays out and the wave crashes on the beach.'

The truth as it is known in the trenches is not always in accordance with the 'black book' or legal tomes that some, safely hidden behind them, use to crucify some young police officer, on his own at the coalface in the early hours of a foggy morning with far too many balls in the air and critical urgent decisions to make; often while in personal danger. This bit of truth was lying there on the pathway to be tripped over by the police a few more times yet. The matter continued to build in the media and in the public domain. I provided a number of affidavits to Krebs — by now I had little issue with loyalty as the police hierarchy had shown me none at all.

IN THE END, Pora's case went to the Privy Council in London — then New Zealand's final legal authority — for what would be the last time. My affidavit, along with those from others, was presented at the last Privy Council hearing in 2014. The decision was released in March 2015 and was unsurprising. The conviction of Teina Pora was overturned and sent back to New Zealand with a recommendation that Pora not be put on trial again. The

Commissioner of Police apologised to Teina Pora, who received millions of dollars for his 21-year stay in prison.

I look back almost in disbelief that the only time a brief from me has gone to the Privy Council, it was not for the prosecution. In the final assessment, owing to a Crown challenge, the Privy Council did not accede to my evidence or similar evidence from a Professor Owens, then a professor of psychology at the University of Auckland. Regardless, the result was inevitable. It ended as it was always going to end, through all the years of the police hierarchy digging themselves a deeper hole. The wave had now crashed on the shore with not an iota of saving grace for the police.

The matter was now shelved. Following severe criticism from all quarters of the justice system, the media, rape victims, Susan Burdett's family, and everyone who loves to kick the police as a sport . . . it was filed. I never heard a word from anyone in the police hierarchy to acknowledge that I had been right and they had been in the wrong. I did not imagine there would be an apology, but I thought that at least there might have been some acknowledgement that not only had I been hung out to dry, but also all the work — even the very existence — of the Criminal Profiling Unit had been potentially endangered. But nothing. This lack of even an acknowledgement of how this travesty of justice could have dragged on so long was yet another disappointing response from an employer that I now had served for over 46 years.

No review. Subject closed — or was it? There was still Rewa. With Pora's murder conviction quashed and, consequently, his presence at the Susan Burdett murder scene removed, was there now a hope, a chance, to convict the Lone Wolf, the rapist we all knew had murdered Susan Burdett?

IN LATE 2017, Teina Pora was still attracting media attention regarding his rightful cash payout for wrongful imprisonment. Not something that involved me at all; it was something I left to the experts.

Then there came a call — from the public, the justice system, police, the Burdett family and the media — for Rewa to be re-tried for the murder of Susan Burdett. Now this interested me, as it had done for over twenty years. Unburied business always has a bad smell about it.

Most of the comments made by legal types seemed to be that once there had been a stay of proceedings (such as that following the first two hung-jury trials), it could not be lifted unless there was some new evidence. Well, if the removal of Pora from the murder scene was not a game-changing event, then clearly I was not on the same planet as the legal pundits. Finally, the tide of opinion started to move against Rewa as the dark clouds of doubt and legal stupidity lifted. Rewa was to be tried again, and this time Pora would not be in the way.

A police team was set up just as I was clearing my desk after retiring. I received a phone call from the new 2IC; he was reviewing the evidence and wanted to discuss it with me. I told him to call me after I returned from Europe in two months' time. They had all my affidavits, which contained all they needed to know. And, I'd already been told: 'We know where you stand.' But I was interested to see whether or not they would use me, or my evidence. If I was to use my evidence, I would give it in total; and if I was to be called to give that evidence, then there was to be no handbrake from the Crown. I continued to hear nothing from the police.

Eighteen months later, in early 2019, I went to hear a couple of days of evidence at Rewa's third trial for the murder of Susan

Burdett and met some of the police prosecution team in the corridors of the familiar old Auckland High Court. I told the 2IC that it would be a slam-dunk with Pora out of the mix, but he didn't seem too confident. I didn't know why; surely it was now a given with the obstruction removed?

Included in the Crown's opening address was the following, as reported in the *New Zealand Herald*:

> Rewa's propensity to sexually assault women displayed a
> 'striking resemblance' to the attack on Burdett.
>   In almost all cases the women had the upper parts of
> their body covered, and in almost all of the cases the lower
> half was naked.

It sounded fairly familiar, but there didn't appear to be any mention of Rewa being a lone offender, which was one of the first and most obvious similarities.

I also greeted a couple of our ladies from the original trial, the ones who had spoken at the sexual abuse courses many years earlier. Even after all this time, they still had an interest in this case and were looking for the truth to be finally displayed on behalf of Susan Burdett, their deceased sister in the 'legion of the brave'. It was both an honest and a relentlessly courageous path they had taken. I was amazed to know that the latest police investigation team didn't seem to know who they were, and I introduced them. After all, twenty of our ladies' statements from the 1998 court case formed part of the evidence for this hearing, even if their evidence was not given viva voce this time.

Rewa was a very old-looking guy by now. He clearly had some health issues going on, perhaps due to spending 22 years in the prison system. It was hard to believe that he was the same man, and just a year and one week younger than me. (I didn't know then that cancer was coming my way in a month's time. The criminal might outlive me yet.)

Yet again I was disappointed by the lack of acknowledgement by the police of the work of Phil Taylor, Tim McKinnel, Jonathan Krebs and their team, Michael Bennett (who wrote the book *In Dark Places* about Pora's innocence) and me, who were, after all, responsible for at least giving them a chance to have this day. This day on which they were now patting each other on the back as Rewa was finally, and inevitably, convicted of the murder of Susan Burdett. Had Pora not been removed from the picture, Susan's true murderer would never have been convicted — surely that is what mattered?

Walking from the High Court in February 2019, however, at least it seemed to be finally over — we could all move on, 23 years after Rewa's arrest.

REWA'S LIFE HAS been a catastrophic waste which has brought nothing but harm to others. I remember looking into his eyes in the interview room at Ōtāhuhu back in 1996. He was menacing, confrontational, challenging, uncompromising, dangerous. Yet also intelligent, confident and knowing. A sad and very bad man, but certainly not a mad one.

Clearly Rewa had suffered in childhood, after his mother died when he was a baby, and this was followed by abandonment and neglect at an early age. Regardless, the road he chose was far too long for him to ever find his way back now, even if he wanted to. Although in the 2019 trial Rewa was physically weaker, I saw no sign of any softening in his demeanour. The same remorseless eyes bored out at the court — still knowing and uncompromising, but I sensed that he knew he had lost. Despite this, he resolutely refused to surrender, pleading not guilty — the Lone Wolf facing down the world one last time: 'I will take you all on by myself.'

He never admitted to anything he didn't have to. He pleaded guilty only to the attacks where there was DNA and the victims were alive to challenge any explanations of his, as opposed to Susan Burdett who was not alive to challenge his story. He pleaded guilty to the charges he had no hope of defending against, purely to gain some advantage during the trials. A forlorn hope for him, as it turned out. Rewa was sentenced to life imprisonment for Susan Burdett's murder, to be served concurrently with his previous 22-year preventive detention sentence for his multiple rapes.

I am sure that Rewa still has many other secrets hidden behind the narcissistic veneer that serves to disguise a disintegrated and disjointed personality, reflected in the macabre ritual played out in his attacks. He is not solely a brutal violent man who raped whenever he felt like it. There is much more behind that mask; if he were to remove the mask, and had the right guide to help him to crawl out from behind it, he would free the others whom he surely offended against — both the crimes we didn't charge him with, and others we don't know about. But letting anyone else into his secret world is unlikely to ever happen. I believe he will shuffle off from this world without a care for any of his many victims.

In February 2023, Malcolm Rewa's bid for a fourth trial for the murder of Susan Burdett was dismissed. He never pleaded guilty to the murder or rape of Susan Burdett, instead fighting it right to the end, through three trials. This was his right, but it did show that he had no acceptance, remorse or compassion for those whom he offended against. There is a well-known saying: 'Wolves don't lose sleep over the opinion of sheep.' There stands the Lone Wolf.

Rewa is one of the few offenders who should never be released. He sits out his time, alone, in Pāremoremo high-security prison. He might have thought he was too smart to be brought down to life in a single cell, but when you try to run from your demons it is a race you will never win. They will catch you, sooner or later. This demon was caught by the legal system. Finally.

REFLECTIONS

DURING THE COURSE OF MY career, I reviewed and behaviourally profiled all of New Zealand's known serial and well-known rapists, both active and historical. These dozens of men included many whose cases I had been involved with. There were also some offenders whose crimes I did not deal with personally, such as the Parnell Panther rapist and the Beast of Blenheim.

Sometimes early in your career you meet villains who later become national horrors, and this can be embarrassing. One such incident took place in about 1974, while I was making inquiries in Manurewa as a uniformed officer. On the Friday afternoon, a smelly little man who reminded me of Ratty from *The Wind in the Willows* came in to the patrol base with a sad story of arriving in Manurewa with his bride-to-be but without their two witnesses, who had not arrived. Ratty whined that he knew no one else in Manurewa and the vicar was waiting in a flat up the road for the marriage to take place. He had suggested that Ratty go to the police station to see if we could carry out the witnessing duties in this time of urgent need. Ratty presented his fiancée, who seemed very keen to marry this smelly individual, so I agreed to attend along with one other officer. The marriage duly took place, and on Ratty's insistence we had to be photographed with the happy couple.

A few weeks later Ratty was caught by night-shift staff after a prowling incident. With little evidence to connect him to the offence and on showing them his photograph with me and the other local police officer, he was allowed to go home. When I heard about this, I knew instantly that there was more to Ratty than I had first imagined. Sometime later, an old cadet room-mate of mine, 'the Fox' Fletcher, called at the patrol base with a big CIB file relating to bigamy; much to his enjoyment, I was a signatorial witness to this event. Ratty was subsequently convicted of this offence, along with other sexual crimes.

Much later, while reviewing the cases of serious national sexual offenders, I analysed one Colin Wilson; indeed a very mixed-up and violent repeat sexual offender. But it was not until my retirement as a sworn officer in 2007 that I was to learn from the Fox that Ratty — aka Colin Wilson — was in fact the Beast of Blenheim. The irony, of course, was that I had spent most of the previous fifteen-odd years analysing the behaviour of just such offenders. To be duped by the Beast early in my career was something I just had to suck up.

COMMON TO ALL the very serious offenders I profiled were backgrounds of childhood abandonment and neglect, most commonly at a very early age, before the age of seven. So perhaps there is some truth in the dictum 'Give me a boy until he is seven and I will give you the man', variously attributed to Aristotle and a motto of the Jesuits. The abandonment was usually by the father, but the neglect was by both parents. I'll always remember John Banks, former Minister of Police and ex-mayor of Auckland, commenting on one such murderer/rapist, Taffy Hotene, in an interview. 'It goes right back to the family. They have many fathers, sometimes several mothers; they are taken from pillar to post . . . They are like savage dogs; if you tied a dog to a tree in the middle of town, and if everyone who passed it was to kick it, when it was let loose it would bite everything and everyone in sight.'

The lesson here is one of human compassion. If you cannot find that for defendants, then at the very least we should try to understand what created these monsters. If this understanding does not come from simple curiosity, then, as a detective, it should arise from the basic lesson that to understand your prey will help you to identify and find him.

Unfortunately there will always be new Rewas, Thompsons, Kahuis and Reekies crawling out from under the burden of abuse, neglect and abandonment. These disadvantages, coupled with a particular genetic make-up, sets the offender to a task — not unlike the complexity of assembling an Albrecht Dürer-type jigsaw — in an effort to try to hammer his square piece of life's puzzle into a round hole.

When he first appeared at the Ōtāhuhu District Court in 1996, big macho tough man Malcolm Rewa requested a blanket over his head to avoid those who attended in order to abuse him. In contrast, little Joe Thompson, the Ghost, at the same court a year earlier, refused the blanket and looked back at the crowd abusing him; he then pleaded guilty to everything. That told me a lot about the difference between these two men, and what they wanted for the rest of their lives. New Zealand's two worst serial stranger rapists had similarities, but were very different both in personality and in rape signature.

THE TASK OF keeping the peace has become more complicated since 1970. The thin blue line has a more challenging, dangerous and highly visible beat to walk than those of my generation experienced as young officers. However, while the way police carry out their duties may have changed, the goal remains the same. Therein lies the reason why the detective gets up each morning and walks back into the septic tank.

Spending a lot of time in the dark, ugly and brutal areas of our world must surely affect your faith in humanity, or at least how you deal with people in general. The desire to exert power and control is not solely the domain of the rapist; it would appear to simmer below the surface in many others. I learnt this truth first-hand in the trenches.

Most non-police I have spoken to comment about the physical dangers of the job, but don't seem to grasp that the biggest threat to frontline police is the psychological aspect: the effect of the relentless grief, deep sadness, death and damage to the vulnerable that are the daily menu. One of the darkest places I remember my duty taking me to was dealing with sexual abuse in the home (if, indeed, you can call such a place a home). I know these are stories that repeat and repeat, but that doesn't make them any easier to deal with, or to understand, or to cope with.

In one incident, a girl aged around twelve or thirteen had been impregnated by her father, who also gave her an STD. She was placed in the care of the Salvation Army at least until her child was born. At interview, the father was not in the least repentant, acting as if it were his right to rape his own child. To make matters worse, the mother was supportive of her husband and simply abandoned her daughter. Whatever the rationale for this behaviour, it clearly had a very destructive effect on this young girl. She appeared devoid of emotion and robotic in her responses in my interview with her and to all concerned. To this day I cannot help but wonder what kind of future lay ahead of her. Had there been any happy moments in her life so far, any happy places to go back to in those moments before sleep arrives?

My parting gesture was to give her my contact card and ask her to call me if she ever needed help — tomorrow, next month, or at any time in the future. But while others I dealt with over the years did contact me, she never did. She would be 50 now, if indeed she survived at all.

The violation of children is impossible to comprehend when you come from a normal, loving family background. Regardless of how you steel yourself not to become emotionally involved, it is a little like trying to sidestep an avalanche. You walk away with the same feeling of grief as when encountering death. Today there are specialist groups within the police who deal with such offences, such as Puawaitahi established in Grafton, Central Auckland, in 2002. Their staff are never left investigating these crimes for long and they receive regular psychological checks — unheard of when I was in the trenches, when the task of dealing with these horribly dark investigations fell to many of us in general CIB.

The only escape from the evil and profound sadness I encountered was the knowledge that it surfaced in only a few. To be a long-term winner when the teeth of tension are lunching on your arse nearly every day, you have to surround yourself with the right people.

I found the right people, and a true band of brothers and sisters was formed with those who spent many years with me in the dark places, living in rather than just visiting the trenches — no longer the 'young band radiating confidence that our presence would root out the pockets of resistance and widespread evil and intolerance' that we were told about at our graduation parade. But after the daily slog, year in, year out, in the end we on the street knew that we had made a difference to some lives; that we had achieved some closure and some justice for the victims. *This* was what mattered.

I have been privileged to have worked and played in the company of my trench-mates. We may have argued strongly, disagreed with resolve, and shared the darkest moments, but we remain fellow students of the septic tank.

WHEN I RETIRED for the second, and final, time, I was determined that after waltzing between the septic tank and my family for so long, I would leave the septic tank behind once and for all and instead walk among the roses my wife Carolyn and I had planted in our rural retreat. We had moved there after living in my patch eventually became too hard. Although I was fully aware of the importance of knowing your patch and the people living in it, I could never get away from it. Children from local crime families went to school with my children; on the sidelines of sports events I would meet people I had arrested.

While I spent many hours on duty, I always made time to spend with my six children and extended family. I kept as much as I could from them, but of course a lot of the big cases were in the news and my family could not help but be aware. A sports team that one of my sons was in was captained by a man I had just arrested for rape;

my son cleverly changed his surname to avoid any issues with his captain. Another son who attended my first farewell told me he'd learnt more about me and what I'd done that day than he'd ever known. For whatever reason, none of my family ever followed me into the police.

All my service took place in South Auckland, most of it carrying out the duties of a detective and, of course, as a dad. The adventure, the unexpected; the great men and women I worked with; the service I was able to provide to those so vulnerable and those from horrendously violent and abusive backgrounds; the satisfaction that many cases brought — I would do it all again tomorrow (or, at least, most of it).

Chook Henwood
April 2024

ACKNOWLEDGEMENTS

MANY RETIRED POLICE OFFICERS HAVE considered writing about their experiences during their time in the trenches. Most have turned away from the idea because they realised that most of the many memorable moments from their careers, whether good, funny, bad or sad, simply cannot be told in the public arena and are best kept for banter at reunions among those who were present and can best understand them.

But after I found myself stuck at home — first after a round of cancer in 2019, and then during the pandemic — and with encouragement from my wife, Carolyn; a burglar, Dan Dudson; and assisted by a journalist, Phil Taylor, I began writing what turned into a massive 150,000 word rambling voluminous manuscript. Over the next few years much of the content and even concepts changed.

After considering binning the whole idea I sent the ramblings to an editor, Sue Reidy, to see if it was worth continuing with. Sue's enthusiasm and passionate belief in the importance of the story was contagious, and with her encouragement, effort, and direction the ramble halved in size and turned into a potentially publishable prospect.

It was a prospect that Tess Nichol from Allen & Unwin also believed in, putting my story through the publishing process with further work and editing. The result is this book.

Much thanks to Sue for her initial work, and all the Allen & Unwin team: Tess (publisher), Teresa McIntyre (editor), Leonie Freeman (project editor) and no doubt many more who I did not get to meet, firstly for believing in the book, then for scrubbing it up and creating the finishing product.

To ensure accuracy of content I have bounced ideas off or received information from many former (and some still serving) officers including John Manning, Raymond Smith, Russell Lamb, Brian McKenzie, Colin (Mouse) Matthews, Megan Goldie, Timothy Leitch, Mike Bowman, Sherwood Young, Arty Harpur, Rob Rattenbury, Christopher Blake, and Mary Goddard.

Enormous thanks to the Sisters of the Legion of the Brave in Operation Harvey, and L.P. from Operation Park — brave survivors all. Thanks also to Geoff Walker, Jared Savage, Eugene Bingham, Nigel Latta, Trevor Smith, Samantha Lundrigan, Rhonda McHardy, and Jan Jordan.

Thanks to Dan's family and partners, Ruby, Caryn, and Rusty, who have spent time telling their stories, adventures, and the mysteries around this larger-than-life character.

A final thanks to all those who encouraged me to keep going when the journey seemed to be losing its way and I was doubting I could get this done. I am forever grateful for your support.

ABOUT THE AUTHOR

DAVID 'CHOOK' HENWOOD is one of New Zealand's most decorated and respected police officers, having served for 37 years in South Auckland before retiring in 2007. He held the rank of detective sergeant and was awarded a record three silver merit awards during his time as an officer. Now in his early 70s, Henwood has six grown-up children and lives in Cambridge with his wife, Carolyn.